Getting the Point

Getting the Point

A Panic-Free Guide to
English Punctuation for Adults

Jenny Haddon and Elizabeth Hawksley

Floris Books

First published in 2006 by Floris Books
© 2006 Jenny Haddon and Elizabeth Hawksley

British Library CIP Data available

ISBN-10: 0-86315-567-7
ISBN-13: 978-086315-567-3

Printed in Great Britan
By Cromwell Press, Trowbridge

CONTENTS

SYMBOL KEY

♥   personal preference or style

✎   creative writer's tip

✔   correct usage

✘   wrong usage

≡   American usage

💣   careful!

☠   mistakes people make

✏   examples

ACKNOWLEDGMENTS

Thank You ...

Our thanks go to our test pilots Ruth Cohen, Michael Cunningham, William Edmondson, Hugo Hobson, Richard Langley, Richard Saffron, and Jean Woolmer.

Heartfelt thanks also to those who encouraged and supported us in our belief that this book is needed and who helped us bring it to publication: Harriet Bridgeman, Peter Carson, Andrew Hewson, Hilary Johnson, John Matheson, Anne McAllister, Hugo Summerson, Judy West, our patient editor, Christopher Moore, and our illustrator, Harriet Buckley, whose inspired cartoons made us laugh so much.

Foreword

Who needs this book?

— anyone who is worried about their punctuation
— anyone who writes essays
— any parent
— any teacher
— anyone who drafts reports
— anyone who writes business letters
— any manager
— creative writers

For over thirty years punctuation was off the school curriculum. If you are one of those who missed out, this book can help.

Good punctuation helps you to express yourself clearly. It also helps your readers to understand precisely what you meant.

This book is practical. You can just dip in whenever you want to check something particular. Or you can use it to learn how to punctuate from scratch — we take you step by step every inch of the way. We also point out the classic mistakes so that you can avoid them.

We rarely use grammatical terms. We give lots of examples of each punctuation point in our three stories *(Tales of the Whole Nut Café, Dragon Deeds,* and *Casanova on Love)* which we hope will amuse you.

We set out the rules clearly and without jargon; we tell you where there are punctuation options; and we show you how to make the right choice for the impression you want to give.

Good luck!

Chapter One

What is Punctuation?
Sentences and Full Stops

In this chapter we cover:
1. What is punctuation?
2. What is a sentence?
3. What a full stop does
4. How punctuation changes meaning

1. What is punctuation?

When we are talking to someone we do a lot more than hear words. Consider how hard it can be to understand a robot voice. When we listen to real people, as well as the words:

— we *hear the speaker's:*
    tone of voice
    pauses, speeding up and slowing down
    use of emphasis or stress
    hesitation or repetition

— we *see the speaker's:*
    face, with lots of different expressions
    body language, using hands, shoulders, gestures,
    such as a finger pointing or a shrug

— we *ask:*
    questions if something isn't clear

When we're reading, we are not face to face with the writer, so all of these signs are missing. All we have are the signs and letters on the page. No matter what sort of writing you do, you have to help the reader make sense of your words. You can do that by:

— putting your ideas in the right order
— finishing one idea before you start the next
— punctuating to show where ideas begin and end
— punctuating to give a flavour of pauses and expression

2. What is a sentence?

A sentence makes sense on its own. In other words, it tells you something, it asks you something or it exclaims at something.

A sentence always starts with a capital letter. It usually ends with a full stop (.). It may end with a question mark (?) or an exclamation mark (!) instead.

✎ Examples

a) Sex sells.
b) I always look forward to Fridays.
c) Neil always wanted to be an astronaut but, after a massive row with his parents, he gave in and ran the family farm, while reading science fiction in his spare time.

(a) and (b) are very short. (c) is more complicated. Nevertheless, each sentence makes sense on its own.

> 💣 **Careful!**
>
> Can a single word be a sentence? — Yes, it can, sometimes. Think about calling a warning to someone. For example: *Run!* That makes sense on its own.

Quiz 1

Is this a sentence?

Put a full stop at the end if you think it's a sentence.

CASANOVA ON LOVE

1. Don't trust a smooth-talking man
2. Donna Teresa received a love letter
3. If she stepped out on to her balcony at midnight
4. A full moon, as big and bright as a silver plate, shone in at the bedroom window where Donna Teresa was brushing her hair
5. Love, the great deceiver
6. When she heard her father's footsteps, Donna Teresa decided that she
7. Casanova, the famous Italian lover, only seduced ladies who

8. Don Marco, who had challenged Casanova to a duel
9. Always have an alibi ready
10. If you want to seduce someone's wife, always have an alibi ready

(Answers on page 177)

❤ *How long should a sentence be?*

A sentence can be as long or as short as you like. The important thing is to consider your readers. Too many very short sentences and they will feel as if they are on a bus that keeps braking. Sentences that are very long may swamp them.

If you are writing factual reports, it is a good idea to follow the principles of the Plain English Campaign. They say that clear writing has an average sentence length of fifteen to twenty words. We stress that this is an average. Variety keeps the reader's attention.

Creative writers must find their own personal style. Sentence length is part of that. One thought which may be helpful, though: readers pick up rhythm. So, if you are writing an action sequence, you want to keep your sentences short. By contrast, if it is a slow, dreamy moment, long sentences may reinforce the mood. When writing dialogue, remember very few people speak in long sentences. If your character does, then you have already given him a mannerism. Be sure that it is one you want.

Long sentences are good in the right place. We repeat: remember your readers. *The Times* columnist, Bernard Levin, once wrote a whole article that was technically one sentence. It was a joke between him and his readers. They loved it.

3. What a full stop does

As we said, a full stop divides your writing into sentences. It shows where one idea ends and another begins. It helps the reader make sense of the words and it puts your ideas into order. After a full stop, the next word begins with a capital letter.

✎ EXAMPLES

a) All dragons are dangerous some dragons are more dangerous than others.

After reading this, say it aloud. You instinctively drop your voice and pause after the first 'dangerous'. Written with punctuation, this becomes:

All dragons are dangerous. Some dragons are more dangerous than others.

b) Miranda wanted to dye the meringues green for St Patrick's Day Neil thought that was crazy.

With punctuation, this becomes:

Miranda wanted to dye the meringues green for St Patrick's Day. Neil thought that was crazy.

Quiz 2

Making a sentence

Put in full stops and capital letters where necessary.

Dragon Deeds

1. Dragons come in many colours the fiercest are red
2. The dragons at the meeting were specially chosen for their wisdom it took many months to call them all together
3. The baby dragon was laughing so much that he got hiccups he set the bush on fire his father told him sternly not to be so silly
4. Dragons spend all winter burnishing their scales when the ice melts they admire themselves in the mountain lakes
5. The dragons were furious when the eagles came into their valley some of the high council wanted to go to war at once they decided to send Ranulf Forktail to negotiate
6. Norbert easily beat his rival Grimbald in the tail-lashing competition Grimbald was suffering from a strained muscle that year and his tail-lashing was well below his usual standard
7. Snow dragons live among the icy peaks sea dragons live in caves along the shore
8. For many years Matilda won the annual prize for egg-laying this year she got fed up and went off to write an article called *Egg-Laying is a Feminist Issue*
9. When Ranulf had greeted the eagles' herald in the meadow, he went to the eagle camp to meet the leaders they offered him their word beer to help him understand their language

10. Ranulf believed that if you spoke loudly and clearly then everyone would understand Dragonish he refused the word beer

(Answers on page 178)

Quiz 3

Breaking up a piece of writing into sentences

Again, put in full stops and capital letters. You don't need to worry about any other punctuation for the moment. We've done it for you.

Tales of the Whole Nut Café

Neil 'Hopeless-but-he-tries' Findlay
Neil spent several weeks looking for a good place for the Whole Nut Café he found a beautiful shop opposite the lake in the park he was about to sign the lease, when Peaches pointed out that it was a long way from the shopping centre and had very little parking her Jamaican granny always said, 'Men be stupid some-time' so Peaches gave him a checklist and he started again he trawled round the centre looking for a place with parking, accessible to the shops and where there was room to expand upstairs if the Whole Nut Café were successful it had to have room inside to seat at least thirty people plus the counter and they would need room for a decent-sized kitchen at the back with park-ing for deliveries he thought that Peaches was being too picky but he was no good with bossy women he did as he was told

Sundeep

Sundeep walked into the building site that was going to be the Whole Nut Café and asked for a job Peaches was up a ladder so she told Neil to interview him flustered, Neil asked if he had had any previous experience

Sundeep took his hands out of his pockets and said he could do anything cooking ran in his family his Aunty Meera cooked the best samosas north of the border

Neil thought that adding up might be important he asked Sundeep how much change he would need if a customer bought two cups of coffee for 90p each, a slice of cake for £1.10 and a macaroon for 75p and offered a five pound note he rummaged in his briefcase to find his calculator

Sundeep told him not to bother the answer was £1.35

Neil was not sure this was the right answer but Peaches cheered loudly from the top of her ladder he offered Sundeep the job

Ditzy Miranda

Miranda was excited she just knew that an organic café would be brilliant she would wear an unbleached linen smock and perhaps fresh flowers in her hair they would have simple meadow flowers on the tables they could cook with plants, too there was nasturtium salad, dandelion soufflé and rose petal sorbet she poured out her ideas down the telephone to Peaches she was disappointed that her friend did not seem quite as enthusiastic as she was still, she went to bed that night feeling very satisfied

Sensible Peaches

Peaches left her job at the wine bar on Friday everyone had clubbed together to buy her a potted palm for the café they all promised to come and taste her food as soon as the café was up and running

the next morning she was comparing her mother's recipe for Jamaica rum cake using dark rum with her grand-mother's, which used white rum and a lot of muscovado sugar, when the phone rang Miranda hardly let Peaches get a word out before starting to burble about putting flowers in soups and soufflés

she was full of ideas about decorating the food with peonies and petunias, lilac and laburnum she said the food would look gorgeous everyone would be talking about the café

Peaches said that they certainly would laburnum flow-ers were poisonous Miranda was irritated by her lack of vision Peaches raised her eyes to the ceiling and decided on dark rum

(Answers on page 179)

4. Punctuation changes meaning

Full stops are important. All punctuation can change meaning and the full stop, being the longest pause in a continuous piece of writing, can change it crucially.

Compare these two examples of the same words with different punctuation:

a) Bombarded for advice on all sides, Casanova recommended eating fresh fruit to a young lady who complained about spots. He said drinking city water was dangerous.

and:

b) Bombarded for advice on all sides, Casanova recommended eating fresh fruit. To a young lady who complained about spots, he said drinking city water was dangerous.

In (a), Casanova recommends eating fresh fruit to a specific person for a specific purpose. He goes on to tell everyone that drinking city water is dangerous. In (b), he tells everyone to eat fresh fruit but advises only the spotty young lady to avoid city water.

●⁎ Careful!

War and punctuation

In his *Usage and Abusage* (which we heartily recommend) Eric Partridge quotes a telegram received by Dr Jameson, an administrator in the British South Africa Company in 1896. Settlers, mainly British, in the Transvaal were known to be unhappy about taxation when they had no right to vote. Over the border, the South Africa Company was eager to support any uprising — quite apart from points of principle, there were the newly discovered Johannesburg gold fields to be considered. In Bechuanaland, just across the border, Jameson received the following telegram from the settlers:

> It is under these circumstances that we feel constrained to call upon you to come to our aid should a disturbance arise here the circumstances are so extreme that we cannot but believe that you and the men under you will not fail to come to the rescue of people who are so situated.

There is clearly a full stop missing. Jameson interpreted it as being after 'aid': *It is under these circumstances that we feel constrained to call upon you to come to our aid.* Clearly, that means, 'Come at once'.

He could have decided that the full stop was after 'here': *It is under these circumstances that we feel constrained to call upon you to come to our aid should a disturbance arise here.* That obviously means, 'If things get worse, please come', a crucial difference in meaning.

As a consequence of his interpretation, he launched the so-called Jameson Raid, leading 470 troopers over the border, expecting to support a local uprising. The local revolt did not happen. More than thirty of his men died.

Moral: be careful where you put full stops. Lives may depend on it.

Chapter Two

Commas

In this chapter we cover:
1. What is a comma, and what is it for?
2. Commas in a list of things or qualities
3. Commas in a list of actions
4. Commas marking additional information
5. Commas for emphasis
6. Commas after introductory phrases
7. Commas joining sentences with *and* or *but*
8. Commas when addressing somebody or something
9. Commas in personal style

1. What is a comma and what is it for?

A comma (,) separates what you want to say into manageable chunks. You use a comma when you want the reader to pause but you haven't come to the end of an idea.

There are some rules about using commas. We describe these below. There are, however, many instances where the placing of a comma is a matter of personal choice. We look at this in the last section.

If you use them well, commas are particularly helpful when you have to read something out loud, such as lists, minutes of a meeting or the best man's speech at a wedding.

Commas are small but important. Oscar Wilde once jokingly said, 'I was working on the proof of one of my poems all the morning, and took out a comma.'

'And in the afternoon?' he was asked.
'In the afternoon, I put it back again.'

(Quoted in Ralph Keynes, *The Wit and Wisdom of Oscar Wilde*, 1999.)

2. *Commas in a list of things or qualities*

In a list, the comma is used to avoid saying 'and' over and over again. Instead, you use a comma until you get to the very last thing in the list, when you replace the comma with an 'and'.

✎ EXAMPLES

a) Peaches bought flour eggs rum sugar and walnuts.

With commas, this becomes:
    Peaches bought flour, eggs, rum, sugar and walnuts.

b) Norbert was vain egocentric good-looking and full of himself.

With commas, this becomes:
    Norbert was vain, egocentric, good-looking and full of himself.

c) Neil heard the robin a blackbird several thrushes and a blue tit

With commas, this becomes:
    Neil heard the robin, a blackbird, several thrushes and a blue tit.

Take example (a). You could write, *Peaches bought flour and eggs and rum and sugar and walnuts,* but it looks very odd. Normally, you leave out most of the 'ands' and pause after each item to show there's more to come. You use the comma when you want a pause.

However, sometimes you may need to use a comma before the final *and* for clarity.

✐ EXAMPLE

> She went shopping at Harrods, Harvey Nichols, and Marks and Spencer.

Without the comma after Harvey Nichols, it looks as though she is shopping at four shops, one of which is called Marks and one called Spencer.

Quiz 4

Commas in lists of things or qualities

Put in commas where necessary.

Dragon Deeds

1. Matilda decided that laying a large clutch of eggs was boring uncomfortable troublesome and a waste of time for a dragon of her intelligence.
2. Speckled dragons are considered to be honest hard-working reliable tireless and a bit thick.
3. Baby dragons eat heather thistles grubs worms and wasps.
4. A dragon's nest is made of carefully placed branches pine cones sheep's wool pumice and several wolf skins.

5. Albreda's famous word beer needs spring water bats' toe-nails four rock salamanders a pinch of fly-agaric toad-stool and stirring by the light of a full moon for two days sixteen hours forty-two minutes and eight seconds.
6. Sea dragons are blue green iridescent and snake-like.
7. Norbert liked to admire his tail scales teeth horns and reflection in the mountain pools.
8. Breathing out fire requires strong muscles large lungs breath control practice and a good breakfast of hot coals.
9. Underneath his stodgy pompous and bossy exterior Ranulf Forktail was passionate sensitive and rather shy.
10. The dragon chief's funeral was attended by Siberian snow-dragons Atlantic sea-dragons winged horses two unicorns and a phoenix.

(Answers on page 180)

Common usage in the United States includes the final comma before 'and' on every occasion. (In the UK this is known as the Oxford comma because the Oxford University Press also requires it in their house style.) An American example which we like is 'Teachers, Moms, and hoot owls sleep with one eye open'.

💣 Careful!

Sometimes several qualities do not make a list, for example: *The Royal National Lifeboat Society, The International Horticultural Development Association.* These are names or titles, rather than lists. A slightly different example is *the lesser spotted woodpecker* which is what this bird is called. If you then add a description, such as *the rare lesser spotted woodpecker,* you do not need a comma after *rare* as *lesser spotted woodpecker* counts as one term.

3. Commas in a list of actions

As with the list of things, you use a comma until the last two actions which you join with 'and'.

✐ EXAMPLES

a) Miranda tiptoed up the stairs at four in the morning fell into bed turned off the light and was asleep at once

With commas, this becomes:

Miranda tiptoed up the stairs at four in the morning, fell into bed, turned off the light and was asleep at once.

b) Peaches smiled Neil laughed like a drain Sundeep looked puzzled and Miranda cried her eyes out.

With commas, this becomes:

Peaches smiled, Neil laughed like a drain, Sundeep looked puzzled and Miranda cried her eyes out.

Quiz 5

Commas in lists of actions

Put in commas where necessary.

Tales of the Whole Nut Café

1. Peaches photocopied the title deeds took them to her solicitor signed the lease and went to tell the others.
2. Peaches announced that she would cook Miranda would lay the tables Sundeep would wash up and Neil

would deliver his organic vegetables by ten in the morning.

3. Neil's mother came to poke about take stock assess the mess Neil had got himself into this time and offer plentiful advice.

4. Miranda woke up remembered that she had to open the café went back to sleep woke up again and picked up the telephone to call Peaches.

5. Peaches swept the floor several times cleaned the big window rearranged the tables twice and knocked over the big plate of home-made rum cake.

6. Sundeep liked to put on his old jeans borrow his brother's motorbike and ride round the town.

7. Sundeep turned on the old computer waited a few moments pressed the Enter key waited even longer and sighed heavily.

8. Neil drove into town stopped at the traffic lights remembered that he had left the tomatoes on the door-step went three times round the roundabout looking for a gap in the traffic and drove back home again to pick them up.

9. Sundeep told Peaches that he had peeled all the potatoes put out the rubbish sacks for the bin men helped Neil bring in the day's delivery of salad printed the week's menus washed the floor and now he wanted a coffee.

10. Miranda searched through the newspaper found the email address of the tourist officer sent him a message prowled round the office waiting for his reply pounced on the telephone number at the bottom of his note called him at once and arranged a meeting for the next day.

(Answers on page 181)

4. Commas marking additional information

If you want to add a bit more information about some-body or something, you can do it with a short phrase enclosed by commas. The sentence would still make sense if we left out the words between the commas.

✐ EXAMPLES

a) Casanova, *the famous eighteenth-century Italian lover,* liked his housemaids to be young and attractive.
b) Maria, *his pretty laundry maid,* wished he'd keep his hands to himself.
c) He chased her round the linen room, *which was secluded at the end of the corridor,* and manoeuvred her towards a pile of blankets, *conveniently piled up in a corner.*

Note that when the short phrase comes at the end of the sentence, the phrase must end with a full stop, as in (c).

Quiz 6

Commas marking additional information

Put in commas where necessary.

Dragon Deeds

1. Ermintrude the oldest dragon kept her voice in trim by yodelling every morning.
2. Albreda famous for her word beer prided herself on her head for drink.
3. Norbert the winner of the tail-lashing competition was too vain to be a popular dragon.

4. I Matilda do hereby declare that I am standing for election to the Dragon Council.

5. Ranulf Forktail the dragons' negotiator went to see Og king of the eagles.

6. Beltane the dragons' spring festival was celebrated with a huge bonfire which was the result of many weeks' preparation.

7. The visiting dragon who was a beautiful emerald green said that he was named Tamerlane after a famous king and that he came from Sogdiana a country thousands of miles away.

8. The council meeting comprised Grimbald the fire breathing expert Matilda the anti-egg campaigner and Ranulf the chief negotiator.

(Answers on page 182)

Casanova thinks of her as 'the-lady-who-danced-beautifully'.

● Careful!

Commas are used to mark off additional information. However, sometimes information introduced by words like *who, which, whose, that,* is not additional but essential because it defines the thing you are talking about. In that case there are no commas.

⬦ EXAMPLE

> As the dancing master had told Casanova, the class was full of awkward country girls, a few stiff older ladies and just one truly natural dancer. As he propped himself against the wall, watching, the lady *who danced beautifully* smiled at him.

There is no comma marking off *who danced beautifully* because it defines the lady among so many others. Casanova thinks of her as 'the-lady-who-danced-beautifully'.

But, in the next example:

> Casanova stalked the new arrival round the ballroom. The mysterious lady, who danced beautifully, smiled at him.

This truly is additional information.

Read the following passage:

> Casanova flirted with so many ladies he could not even remember all their names. There was the lady who smiled at him on the steps of St Mark's. There was the pretty daughter of a merchant, who sang out of tune.

29

However, the lady whom he invited to the ridotto was his favourite. She had a naughty twinkle, which seemed to light up the room.

Why we have and have not used commas in this passage:

Casanova flirted with so many ladies he could not even remember all their names.

(No comma after *ladies* because essential information follows to complete the sense.)

There was the lady who smiled at him on the steps of St Mark's.

(No comma before *who* because it introduces essential information to distinguish the lady from among so many.)

There was the pretty daughter of a merchant, who sang out of tune.

(Comma before *who* is a signal that 'who sang out of tune' is additional information about the pretty daughter. Without the comma, it would mean that it is the merchant who sang out of tune.)

However, the lady whom he invited to the ridotto was his favourite.

(No comma before *whom* because, again, it introduces essential information to distinguish the lady from among so many.)

She had a naughty twinkle, which seemed to light up the room.

(Comma before *which* because it tells us more about the 'naughty twinkle'.)

30

5. Commas for emphasis

Commas are also used to separate such words or phrases as *however, in fact, of course, therefore, nevertheless, naturally, actually, additionally, too, as you know,* when these words are used as road signs to the reader. They may point out a cause or a contradiction. Often they underline that something is unusual or funny. The sentence would still make sense if we left out the words between the commas but the reader would not necessarily understand it the way the writer wants.

✐ EXAMPLES

a) Casanova, of course, invited the Countess to have a glass of wine at his palazzo.
b) The Countess, however, said that she wanted an early night.
c) Casanova, therefore, escorted her home like a gentleman and made love to her in his gondola.

Some people think that commas can be scattered all over a page like pepper over a pizza. But that's no good if they don't make your meaning clear. So when you place commas, it's to make clear exactly what you mean.

✐ EXAMPLES

a) Casanova said that of course he would be discreet and see her safely home.
b) However attractive he was, the lady had been warned against him by her friend, Caterina, amongst others.
c) Caterina, too, had said he was ruthless but in the end the Countess found him too alluring to resist.

31

Quiz 7

Commas for emphasis

Put in commas where necessary.

Tales of the Whole Nut Café

1. Neil was in fact hopeless at adding up the till receipts correctly.
2. Miranda had been warned about cooking too much. Nevertheless she was so excited about her four-cheese scones with added sage that she made far more than she'd intended.
3. Sensible Peaches of course made Neil sit down and draw up a proper business plan.
4. Neil naturally felt that men knew best so he ignored Peaches's advice on the grounds that the Bank Manager was a friend of his father.
5. The Bank Manager however told Neil that he couldn't sanction a bank loan without a proper business plan.
6. Miranda as you know is a bit of an air head but she has a good heart.
7. We shall have to see therefore if the Whole Nut Café can open on time.
8. Sundeep knew that Peaches was reluctant to experiment with his Aunty Meera's recipe for samosas. All the same he kept trying to persuade her.

(Answers on page 183)

6. Commas after introductory phrases

A comma is used after an introductory remark or idea to let the reader know that the main subject of the sentence is still to come. Introductory phrases put the main subject into a context *before* it arrives in the sentence. They can be anything from a single word to several words, or right up to a major thought.

(i) Single introductory words are very like emphasis (see above) and use the same signal words:

✐ EXAMPLES

> Naturally, Casanova promised to see her the next day.
> Meanwhile, the Countess had a plan of her own.

(ii) You can have a short introductory phrase of several words before you get to the main sentence:

✐ EXAMPLES

> Feeling mildly piqued, the Countess determined to ask Casanova to escort her to a masked ball and to send her maid in her place.
> Pleased with her plan, she wrote to him the moment she got back to her palazzo that night.

(iii) Sometimes an introductory phrase can be very long. If it doesn't make sense on its own, it needs a comma to mark the break rather than a full stop.

✐ EXAMPLES

> While he was surprised to receive a letter from the Countess so soon after their farewell, Casanova was intrigued by the invitation.

33

As if she were in a dream, the Countess watched the moonlit canal and waited for his reply.

7. Commas joining sentences with and or but

Sometimes you want to join two complete thoughts (sentences) together. One way to do so is to use a joining word such as: *for, and, nor, but, or, yet, so.* If you do that, it is correct to put a comma before the joining word. However, nowadays people tend to leave out this comma if one of the thoughts being joined together is quite simple. What you do will depend on personal taste and national usage.

✐ EXAMPLES

Read the two following sentences:

> Casanova broke the seal of the letter with his stiletto.
> A scented rose petal fluttered to the floor.

Joined together, these become:

> Casanova broke the seal of the letter with his stiletto, and a scented rose petal fluttered to the floor.

The two thoughts are not complicated. One action follows the other immediately. Only one person is involved. A modern writer would probably choose to leave out the comma.

> The servant girl confided to her mistress that Casanova was pursuing her.
> The Countess suggested that they set a trap for him.

Joined together, these become:

> The servant girl confided to her mistress that
> Casanova was pursuing her, and the Countess
> suggested that they set a trap for him.

Here the two ideas are more complex. The actions take some time. Two people are involved. All this indicates we should use a comma to separate the two thoughts.

> The Countess was furious with herself for sending
> Casanova a love letter filled with rose petals.
> She swore revenge.

Joined together, these become:

> The Countess was furious with herself for sending
> Casanova a love letter filled with rose petals and
> swore revenge.

Although the actions here are complex and take place over time, the Countess does them both. We do not even need to repeat 'the Countess' for the second action. We don't want the reader to pause between the two actions. All this indicates you should not use a comma.

> Casanova arrived early at the rendezvous.
> The masked figure was already there.

Joined together, these become:

> Casanova arrived early at the rendezvous, but the
> masked figure was already there.

☠ Mistakes People Make: comma splicing

Are you a comma freak? People often use commas where they should use full stops, especially in emails. This is called 'comma splice'. It can give the impression that the writer is in a breathless rush. It is also very informal. If you are writing a letter applying for a job, a prospective employer will not be impressed by a gush of words.

What impression do you have of the person who wrote this email to a famous novelist?

> My name is Belinda Bubblewit, I have written a novel set in the Restoration, I love all kinds of historical fiction, especially cavalier and roundheads, cavaliers are so sexy, aren't they? My book is about half finished, that's time to talk to an agent, I thought, so I wondered if, as a published novelist, you knew anyone I could approach, not that I'm asking for a personal introduction or anything, just a name, I'd like to send something off before I go on holiday at the end of the month, I am so excited about this project, I can't wait to get feedback on it, many thanks for your help, Belinda.

Are you surprised that the published novelist couldn't help?

Another point to remember is that too many commas make it difficult for the reader to follow the sense, especially when they are used instead of full stops.

A comma freak has written the following story:

> The woman in the mask turned, slipped away silently, Casanova gathered his cloak about him and ran after her, the moonlight caught the diamonds on her heels, they sparkled as she ran. ✗

There are a number of ways you could put it right:

> The woman in the mask turned. She slipped away silently. Casanova gathered his cloak about him. He ran after her. The moonlight caught the diamonds on her heels. They sparkled as she ran. ✔

Grammatically this is correct. It is a bit jerky, which may be fine at the start of an action sequence. Alternatively, you might want to consider the following:

> The woman in the mask turned and slipped away silently. Casanova gathered his cloak about him and ran after her. The moonlight caught the diamonds on her heels, and they sparkled as she ran. ✔

This is also correct. It is slower and perhaps more romantic.

To sum up, splicing confuses readers and gives a bad impression. If you want to be a good writer, avoid comma splicing!

8. Commas when addressing somebody or something

A character or the author sometimes speaks directly to someone or something, using their name. In that case the name is separated off from the rest of the sentence by commas. The same applies if the individual's name is replaced by a title (Doctor), a word used in the relationship (mate, dude), an endearment (my love, sweetheart, bunnykins) or even an insult (idiot, you villain).

✐ EXAMPLES

Casanova came into the hall. 'Marco, fetch me my hat, cloak and sword. I'm going out.'

'I have them ready, Signore.'

'I hope to return with Donna Beatrice so don't leave my diary on the table, you rogue, as you did last night.'

Oh Diary, what tales you could tell, thought Marco.

Quiz 8

Commas when addressing someone

Put in appropriate commas when someone or something is being addressed.

CASANOVA ON LOVE

1. 'Donna Lucia you are looking ravishing tonight.'
2. 'That is because I have just become engaged to be married Signor Casanova.'
3. 'You're too late my friend,' said Don Vittorio, coming up. 'The lady is betrothed to me!'

4. 'You mean Don Vittorio that from now on I may only admire her from afar?'
5. 'I know your reputation Casanova. I forbid you to approach my future wife.'
6. Casanova thought, we'll see about that my friend.
7. Donna Lucia thought, Vittorio you are rich, noble and have just given me a vastly expensive diamond ring but Casanova is far more attractive than you poor toad.
8. Don Vittorio thought, I'm not sure Lucia that I entirely trust you.
9. Oh Love how much stronger you are than Honour!

(Answers on page 184)

9. *Commas in personal style* ❤

The best way of learning to punctuate is to read good writers. Having said that, however, it is true that what is considered good style has changed enormously in the last two hundred years.

When Jane Austen was writing around the beginning of the nineteenth century, the Educated Man (for it nearly always was a man) had been to one of a handful of universities and studied classics. As a result, good style was full of long sentences and Latinate phrasing. This required lots of punctuation and especially commas.

In the twentieth century, Ernest Hemingway wrote the classic novel *For Whom the Bell Tolls* and managed to get rid of commas almost entirely. He shortened his sentences to the simplest possible structures in order to do so. He also used a lot of direct speech (people speaking).

Jane Austen and Ernest Hemingway

A comparison

'There was a momentary expression in Captain
Wentworth's face at this speech, a certain
glance of his bright eye, and curl of his hand-
some mouth, which convinced Anne, that
instead of sharing in Mrs Musgrove's kind
wishes, as to her son, he had probably been
at some pains to get rid of him; but it was too
transient an indulgence of self-amusement to be
detected by any who understood him less than
herself; in another moment he was perfectly
collected and serious, and almost instantly after-
wards coming up to the sofa, on which she and
Mrs Musgrove were sitting, took a place by the
latter, and entered into conversation with her,
in a low voice, about her son, doing it with so
much sympathy and natural grace, as shewed
the kindest consideration for all that was real
and unabsurd in the parent's feelings.'

(Jane Austen, *Persuasion*)

'I was tired of rum St James without thinking
about it. Then the story was finished and I was
very tired. I read the last paragraph and then I
looked up and looked for the girl and she had
gone. I hope she's gone with a good man, I
thought. But I felt sad.'

(Ernest Hemingway, *A Moveable Feast*)

40

The effect is staccato and deadpan. Of course, emotions seethe underneath, as indeed they do with Jane Austen, but the tone and effect of both writers is quite different.

As we said in Chapter 1 (page 13), factual writing, for example in business and journalism, is better in short sentences. Short sentences mean fewer commas. Legal documentation used to have longer sentences and no commas because of the comma's capacity to change meaning!

In creative writing, action scenes are usually written with shorter sentences and few commas. If you want to be more lyrical, however, the comma, properly used, will help you interweave your ideas like a tapestry. The more subtle, witty and sophisticated you want to be, the more likely you will be to find commas essential.

To find your personal style:

— Write the first draft as if you were speaking to someone.
— Read it.
— Check that you have included the commas which this chapter suggests are necessary.
— Get rid of commas which reflect the mistakes we have outlined.
— Read it again.
— Check for clarity. If you need to change a comma (or any other punctuation) to make something crystal clear, do it.
— Read it again. Does it have the right tone?
— Adjust commas (or other punctuation) to give the right flavour to your writing.

Commas for the American reader

Spoken American English often emphasizes different words from spoken British English. Does it matter where punctuation is concerned? Popular US author Anne McAllister writes: 'Punctuation in the US is somewhat different from the UK. I can tell you this from my confusion upon reading letters and books. You use a lot less punctuation than we do. We use it all over the place in letters, and we use commas *lots* more frequently in books. I am forever having to go back and re-read sentences in English (UK) books to figure out what the hell they're talking about.'

When you are checking for clarity and tone, always ask yourself what your reader will understand most clearly.

Chapter Three

Apostrophes

In this chapter we cover:
1. What is an apostrophe?
2. Left-out letters
3. Ownership
4. *Its* and *it's*

1. What is an apostrophe?

This is an apostrophe ('). (Pronounced, a-*poss*-tro-fee.)

It is used mainly in two ways:
— to show that a letter or letters have been left out
— to show ownership

2. Left-out letters

An apostrophe shows where a letter or letters are deliberately left out.

✎ EXAMPLES

don't instead of *do not*
won't instead of *will not*
I'm instead of *I am*
they've instead of *they have*
it's instead of *it is* or *it has*
the postman's coming instead of *the postman is coming*

As you can see, these examples come from spoken language. These shortened words, known as 'contractions', are very common and we all know them and use them. Although contractions like those above are common in speech, it is best to avoid them in formal writing such as business letters, academic work, and so on.

Less common examples of contractions are poetic words such as *e'er* for *ever* and dialect pronunciation such as *'appen* instead of *happen* or *'ee* instead of *thee* or *rockin'* instead of *rocking*.

Quiz 9

Left-out letters

Leave out letters and put in apostrophes.

The sentences below are formal. Make them more like everyday speech by using contractions as in the examples above.

Dragon Deeds

1. 'I am the oldest dragon here,' said Ermintrude. 'I should not have to wait.'
2. If you are entering the dragon tail-lashing competition, you will need to practise regularly.
3. It is unusual for dragons to fall ill. Normally they are very healthy.
4. 'Come along, there is just time for claw-clipping before supper,' said Albreda to her grandson. 'Will not,' he replied rudely.
5. He had always hated having his claws clipped. He would rather miss supper than have them done.

6. 'We have not had a good year,' said Ranulf Forktail. 'Only six eggs were laid, though, fortunately, they have all hatched.'

7. 'I have got better things to do than sit on eggs,' snapped Matilda. 'You will not catch me doing it again.'

8. Ranulf could not think of a suitably crushing reply, so he muttered, 'You have got a nerve,' in a weak way, and snorted.

(Answers on page 184)

3. Ownership

An apostrophe follows another word to show possession or ownership.

✐ EXAMPLES

Matilda's eggs	means	*the eggs belonging to Matilda*
A dragon's wings	means	*the wings of a dragon*
Peaches's plan	means	*the plan that Peaches thought of*
The girl's café	means	*the café owned by the girl*
The book's cover	means	*the cover of the book*

The *'s* means that the subject owns something, in one way or another.

How to use an apostrophe:

(i) When the owner's name ends in 's':

✐ EXAMPLES

St James's Square
the bus's route
Peaches's plans

45

♥

Some authorities tell you to leave off the final -s in certain circumstances, for instance, if it is silent, especially in names ending in –us or –es.

✐ EXAMPLES

    Jesus' teaching ✔
    Jesus's teaching ✔
    the teaching of Jesus ✔

    Peaches' ideas ✔
    Peaches's ideas ✔
    the ideas of Peaches ✔

    Dickens' novels ✔
    Dickens's novels ✔
    the novels of Dickens ✔

Our advice is to check the house style of your employer, college or publisher. If you have a choice, do whatever you think will be clearest for the reader. Once you have made a choice, be consistent. If you prefer to avoid using the form altogether, you can usually recast the phrase e.g. *the novels of Dickens, the doves of Venus.*

(ii) When you have more than one owner:

Normally to make a plural you add 's' or 'es' for example, *frog, frogs; bus, buses.* Then the apostrophe goes after the final 's' of the plural.

✐ EXAMPLES

the girls' café	means	*the café belonging to the girls*
mountain dragons' wings	means	*the wings of the mountain dragons*
shops' signs	means	*the signs belonging to the shops*
buses' routes	means	*the routes of the buses*

(iii) When it is an unusual plural:

There are a few exceptions where there is no added -*s* in the plural. We set out some of the most common below.

✐ EXAMPLES

child	children	children's books
woman	women	women's shoes
man	men	men's expectations
mouse	mice	mice's tails

You will see that in both (ii) and (iii), first we make the plural, then we indicate ownership.

(iv) When you have more than one owner who is named:

Use the apostrophe with the last name only, as long as they share ownership.

Ben and Jerry's Ice Cream
Neil, Peaches, Miranda and Sundeep's café
The Army and Navy's plan

💣 Careful!

But owners may not share ownership! In that case you would say:

Grimbald's and Ranulf's wings
The Army's and Navy's budgets

💣 Careful!

Sometimes the thing owned is missing because it is obvious.

✐ EXAMPLES

I went to Maria's on Saturday.

The word 'house' is obvious after Maria's, so we don't say it.

Daniel's wine was lovely but I really didn't like Ben's.

Again, the word 'wine' is obvious after 'Ben's', so we don't say it.

☠ Mistakes People Make: wrong apostrophes

Now you know the rules, you can enjoy yourself collecting examples of wrong uses of the apostrophe. It is certainly unfair but it is so easy to collect stall holders' notices (often called the Greengrocers' Apostrophe) saying things like Cauliflower's or, even more bewilderingly, Tom's £1 a bag, which presumably means a bag of tomatoes costs £1.

Quiz 10

Ownership

Put in apostrophes where necessary.

Tales of the Whole Nut Café

1. Sundeeps idea of cleaning was to sweep any rubbish under the counter.
2. The Whole Nut Cafés walls were painted primrose yellow.

3. If Mirandas mother was a fuss-pot, Neils was far worse.
4. Mirandas recipe for ice-cream was superior to Peachess.
5. The womens cloakroom had fluffy pink towels.
6. Miranda and Peachess specialities included avocado with honey and mustard dressing.
7. The customers coats were hung on a pair of antlers which Sundeep had found in a skip.
8. Peachess secret dream was to bath in asses milk.
9. Neil missed the meeting because he was at the Mens Singles Final at Wimbledon.
10. Sundeep was a great success as a clown at the childrens party and Mirandas hedgehog-shaped cake was eaten to the last crumb

(Answers on page 185)

4. *It's and its*

It's means *it is* or *it has*.

✐ EXAMPLES

— *It is raining* can be shortened to:
    It's raining
— *I think it is a good idea* can be shortened to:
    I think it's a good idea
— *It has gone on long enough* can be shortened to:
    It's gone on long enough.

Its, without an apostrophe, is used only to show ownership. *Its* belongs to the group: *his, her, your, our, their.*

📖 EXAMPLES

> The cat licked his face.
> The cat licked her ear.
> The cat licked its fur.
> Sundeep had lost his mobile phone.
> Peaches had lost her handbag.
> The cookery book had lost its last page.

Equally the ownership words *his, hers, ours, yours, theirs,* never take an apostrophe.

📖 EXAMPLES

> Casanova saw that the lady was his for the asking.
> The dropped handkerchief was hers.
> She whispered softly, 'Which gondola is ours?'
> He said, 'I am yours.'
> The night was theirs and they used it well.

☠ Mistakes People Make: *it's* and *its*

It is a common error to write sentences like: *The cat licked it's fur.* ✗

So why is this wrong? — Because *it's* means *it is.*

We don't write: *The cat licked it is fur.* ✗

The correct sentence should be: *The cat licked its fur.* ✔

Its is an ownership word just like *his, her, our* or *their.* It doesn't need an apostrophe.

Quiz 11

It's or its?

Put in either *it's* or *its* as appropriate in the following sentences.

CASANOVA ON LOVE

1. If a lady is early for an assignation,   a bad sign.
2.   a pleasing courtesy to send flowers to a lady the morning after.
3. The morning can bring   regrets.
4. If a lady sends a note,   contents may be deceptive.
5. In taking a romantic stroll,   always advisable to ensure that the lady's pet dog is on   lead.

(Answers on page 186)

Chapter Four

Colons and Semi-colons

In this chapter we cover:
1. What is a colon?
2. What is a semi-colon?

1. What is a colon?

This is a colon (:). A colon is *not* a full stop and so it is not normally followed by a capital letter unless the next word is a proper name e.g. Rome, Neil, Victoria Station, or in a few other special circumstances, set out below.

A colon is used after a general statement to introduce something which says more about it.

✐ EXAMPLES

(i) To introduce more information. This can be a list or simply additional details.

We have the following job vacancies: senior plumber, assistant plumber, two plasterers and an electrician.

Casanova was a deeply cultivated man: he introduced the Russian Empress to the music of his friend, Galuppi.

(ii) To introduce a list of headings:

> The causes of the First World War were: the decline of the Ottoman Empire, the rise of militarism in Germany, border disputes with France and aspirations to nationhood in the Balkans.

This is particularly useful for setting out the contents of an academic essay.

(iii) To introduce a quotation:

> As Maryon Pearson said: 'Behind every successful man there's a surprised woman.'*

* Maryon Elspeth Pearson (1902–1991) wit, wife of Lester Pearson, fourteenth Prime Minister of Canada

(iv) In a business format, following words such as:
To: From: Date: Re: Invoice: — You will notice
that these are followed by a capital letter.

To: Neil
From: Peaches
Re: Leaking roof

(v) Sometimes in titles of books or articles:

Through Mere and Fen: A Suffolk Love Story
Churchill: The War Years

Quiz 12

Colons

Put in a colon where appropriate.

Dragon Deeds

1. There are many different sorts of dragons Siberian
   snow dragons, Atlantic sea dragons, domestic speckled dragons and rare Caledonian blue dragons.
2. The Dragon Council Agenda was as follows apologies
   for absence, agreeing the minutes of the last meeting,
   report on the decline in egg-laying, security for the
   Beltane Festival, and any other business.

   (Note the Oxford comma here, after Beltane
   Festival and before the final 'and', which we have
   put in for clarity. See Chapter 2, page 24.)
3. Matilda gave a list of her forthcoming articles 'Egg-
   laying is a Feminist Issue'; 'She-Dragons' Manifesto';
   'Ermintrude A Life of Contrasts'; and 'Tail-lashing
   for Females'.

4. Memo

   To Og, King of the Eagles

   From   Ranulf Forktail

   Re River boundary

5. The causes of Grimbald's accident whilst fire-breathing
   were the following over-eating hot coals that morning,
   a strong westerly wind and poor maintenance of the fire
   extinguishers.

6. As Albreda's little rhyme had it

   > A glass of word beer
   > Will make meaning clear.
   > Too much of the brew
   > And the meaning's askew.

7. Tamerlane's address 42, Temple Way, Samarkand,
   Sogdiana.

8. Ermintrude's catchphrase was I can remember the
   time when speckled dragons knew their place.

9. For tickets for the tail-lashing competition contact Athelstan Silverwing, Ermintrude Glop or the
   Administrator, Retirement home for Gentle-dragons.

10. Events at the Beltane Festival will include fire-jumping,
    rock-hurling, a special performance of the Caledonian
    Dragons' Moon Dance and the first-years' wing-flapping
    competition.

(Answers on page 187)

2. What is a semi-colon?

This is a semi-colon (;). A semi-colon is less of a pause than a full stop but more than a comma.

The job it does is to separate statements within a sentence. These statements could almost stand alone. However, because they have something to do with each other, the writer wants to show them standing together. In many cases, using semi-colons is very much a matter of personal style.

✐ EXAMPLES

(i) To make a contrast between two ideas:
 Airport novels will last for a season; Jane Austen's *Pride and Prejudice* has been in print for a hundred and eighty years.

(ii) To set out a series of ideas related to a single theme:
 The causes of the First World War were: a) the decline of the Ottoman Empire; b) the rise of militarism in Germany; c) border disputes with France; d) aspirations to nationhood in the Balkans.

Here, a colon is used first, followed by phrases separated by semi-colons. You will remember we gave a similar example above (page 54) to show how a colon is used.

The wizard told the children they had three tasks before they could go home: Sarah had to find a compass; Ben had to find the Lion Gate; and Daniel had to find the courage to lead them through the Wild Wood.

Often the ideas in a list like this could stand as single sentences. The writer chooses to group them with semi-colons in order to show that they are closely connected to a single main idea.

You may ask what is different about a list with semi-colons compared with a list separated by commas. A list with commas is usually simple. If you want to write a list of more complicated ideas, then a semi-colon is better. Remember, the semi-colon tells you to pause for longer. With a list of more complicated ideas, you have to give the reader a longer breathing space.

(iii) To set out a much looser set of ideas about a single theme:

On the evening that the Queen of Sheba arrived there were trumpeters dressed in scarlet damask blowing their hearts out; loose-haired girls in flowing muslin robes scattering rose petals before her; four and twenty camels carrying her gifts for King Solomon; statesmen scurrying; servants serving; dancers dancing; and the paparazzi.

Quiz 13

Semi-colons

Put in a semi-colon where appropriate.

Tales of the Whole Nut Café

1. Neil's mother said it was a pity that Peaches dressed like a tart and couldn't speak the Queen's English

Arabella Castle dressed like a lady and sounded just
like the Duchess of Bywater.

2. Peaches realized that Neil could be quite cool if he cut
his hair if he got rid of that terrible old tweed jacket
with the leather patches on the elbows if he smiled
at her sometimes at management meetings instead of
glowering at his papers all the time if he lightened up,
for heaven's sake.

3. Miranda lost patience and told Neil some home truths:
he fancied Peaches he was too stupid to notice it but
he had fancied her ever since she stood up to him at
that first meeting his mother was always dropping in
to the café to check that he had not asked Peaches out
on a date hadn't he noticed any of that?

4. For the first time Neil really looked at Peaches and
found he liked what he saw: the startling flash of her
big brown eyes the sensuous swish of her red mini
skirt the unexpected clatter of beads in her hair above
all, he liked the sound of her bubbling laughter.

5. Sundeep and Miranda agreed that Neil would be
lucky to escape from Arabella Castle: she asked him
to parties she made her friends ask him to parties she
dropped in when he went to see his mother and if all
that failed, she pulled on her gumboots and stalked
him through his own farmyard.

6. They all said that the café staff did not have time to
help out at the charity picnic but Arabella refused
to accept excuses: not Peaches's work schedule not
Miranda's hot date not even Sundeep's IT skills
course.

7. It was on the picnic that Neil realized what was
going on: finding Arabella sitting beside him every
time he dropped to the grass for a moment his
mother beaming Peaches not meeting his eyes as she

played noisy games with the children, her beaded hair flying, and those unsuitable clothes delectably revealing Arabella swotting a child out of the way as she strode across the cake crumbs to get to him Miranda looking wise and everyone, it seemed, watching him all the time.

8. Neil saw the truth at last: Peaches was frighteningly sexy Arabella was just frightening.

(Answers on page 188)

Chapter Five

Brackets, Hyphens, Dashes and Dots

In this chapter we cover:
1. Round brackets, how and when to use them
2. Square brackets and when to use them
3. Double dashes
4. Single dash
5. Hyphen
6. Dots (ellipsis)
7. Bullet points

1. Round brackets, how and when to use them

Round brackets look like this: (   ). They are sometimes called *parentheses* (pronounced par–*en*–tha–sees).

They are used to insert additional information into a sentence. They come at either end of this additional information, keeping it separate. Brackets always come in pairs; if you have opened a bracket you must close it.

When you use brackets, you are telling the reader that the information marked off in this way is a sort of interruption. It might be of less importance than the main statement or it might be a detail about the main statement. In conversation, it would often be an aside.

Brackets can be useful if your sentence is getting complicated and you want to mark off a piece of information from the rest, to help your reader make sense of the whole.

Do use brackets sparingly, however. If you have too many, it looks as if you did not think properly about the order of your ideas before you started writing and so had to keep interrupting yourself. Also, avoid using brackets within brackets. It looks very messy.

When the information in brackets comes at the end of a sentence, the full stop goes after the closing bracket. If the brackets come in the middle of a sentence, you need no extra punctuation. Sometimes, however, a whole sentence will be inside brackets, in which case the final full stop goes before the closing bracket.

Brackets usually contain:

— a list of examples *or*
— a clarification *or*
— a comment *or*
— an abbreviation *or*
— alternative possibilities *or*
— a reference to information somewhere else.

✎ EXAMPLES

(i) A list of examples:

> The best cottage pies contain a sweet vegetable (carrots, swede, even red peppers) as well as mince, onions and, of course, the mashed potato topping.

(ii) A clarification:

> Don Giovanni reluctantly agreed that Casanova was also a famous lover but pointed out that he (Don Giovanni) was the only one who had seduced a thousand and three women in Spain alone.

(iii) A comment:

> The journey only takes forty minutes by gondola
> (unless it is Casanova taking you home).

(iv) *Sic:*

There is also a special and common use of the brack-eted comment *(sic)*. *Sic* is the Latin for 'thus' meaning 'it really is like this'. It is useful if you want to quote something from another source which you don't believe, which you know is wrong or which is spelled wrongly. It shows the reader that the error is not yours. You are merely reporting what has been written.

> Isabella's mother said that Casanova was a wolf in
> cheap *(sic)* clothing.

> The Vice President said that his party understood
> the importance of bondage *(sic)* between mother
> and child.

As you see, the disclaimer *(sic)* goes immediately after the idea or spelling from which you want to distance yourself.

(v) Abbreviations:

> The International Bank for Reconstruction and Development (IBRD or World Bank) provides advice on major economic restructuring and gives long term finance, up to twenty-five years.

The point of doing this is to explain commonly used initials or shorthand names, in this case for a major international financial institution.

> The Romantic Novelists' Association (RNA) was set up in 1960.

This is a more localized use of a bracketed abbreviation. The point of setting this out is so that throughout the rest of an article or chapter, the Romantic Novelists' Association can be referred to as 'RNA' and the reader will recognize it.

(vi) Alternative possibilities:

> Fill in name(s), age(s) and occupation(s) of your applicant(s) for this programme.

(vii) Referring to information elsewhere:

> Bedrooms are also improved by clever lighting (see section on Lighting).

❤

You can also use brackets in a very informal way to enclose question marks or exclamation marks.

The book will be first published in Europe
(France? Germany?) but is out here in October.

He said he was top of the bill (!) and coming
to London next week.

You see this use of brackets most commonly in personal
emails and quick notes between friends but it can occur
in fiction where the writer is trying to give the impression of rapid writing or intimate notes. If you use it, be
sure that is the impression you want to give. It is best to
avoid this style of brackets in formal writing because it
can come across as careless and even rude.

2. Square brackets and when to use them

These are square brackets [   ]. Square brackets may be
used in the following ways:

(i) To add words to a statement, usually a quotation,
which you, the writer or editor, are putting in for
the sake of clarity. For example:

Today Casanova told me that he went to four masquerades in a week but the evening he remembered
most was with the Contessa [dell'Acqua].

Here the original writer, maybe in his diary, is quite clear
which Contessa he means. But you, quoting from the
diary, want to make sure that your reader knows it is the
Contessa dell'Acqua.

Another example is when you shorten a quotation by cutting something out. You may then need to put in something new, typically someone's name, to make the meaning clear.

> Og, King of the Eagles, met the dragons under
> Ranulf Forktail in a battle zone which was more
> suited to the eagles than their opponents but ...
> [Og] failed to take full advantage of this.

(ii) Formally in academic and legal writing to add information to what is already enclosed within round brackets. For example:

> Baker concluded that it would be impossible for the
> liquid to be totally absorbed at room temperature.
> (These results have since been overturned by fur-
> ther experiment [see Halling and Baker, 2004].)

Note: You have to close the square brackets before you put in the punctuation required within the round brackets, in this case a full stop.

(iii) To show ideas added to a work later, either by the original author or an editor:

> Hamilton arrived in London in the spring or sum-
> mer of 1850. [October 1850. Ed.]

(iv) To give the reader page references:

> [continued on page 5, column 6]

(v) To show translations of titles in academic work:

> *Religio Medici* [The Religion of a Doctor]

Although mainly used for serious purposes, and hardly at all by popular writers, square brackets can be used to play games with readers. The magazine *Private Eye* has immortalized them with its regular ironic comment within articles by an imagined drunken editor: *[Shome mishtake shurely — Ed.]*

3. Double dashes

These are double dashes: (—   —).

Double dashes (known as em-dashes in your word processing package) are used in a similar way to brackets to give additional information. Dashes are less formal than brackets, so are particularly suited to any piece of writing that tries to give the feeling of speech. They cannot, however, be used to do all the jobs that brackets do. Dashes are mainly used to contain:

— a list of examples *or*
— a clarification *or*
— a brief descriptive gloss *or*
— a comment *or* sometimes
— a reference to information held somewhere else

✐ EXAMPLES

(i) A list of examples:

> The best cottage pies contain a sweet vegetable — carrots, swede, even red peppers — as well as mince, onions and, of course, the mashed potato topping.

(ii) A clarification:

> Don Giovanni reluctantly agreed that Casanova was also a famous lover but pointed out that he — Don Giovanni — was the only one who had seduced a thousand and three women in Spain alone.

(iii) A comment:

> The journey only takes forty minutes by gondola — unless it is Casanova taking you home — and, if you pay extra, the gondolier will sing all the way.

(iv) Referring to information elsewhere:

> Bedrooms are also improved by clever lighting — see section on Lighting — and subtle use of colours.

4. Single dash

This is a single dash (—). The single dash is used to signal a break in thought or speech. The break tends to be abrupt, rather than trailing off.

> Casanova prowled behind Isabella's chair, leaned over to touch her neck and — The door banged back on its hinges. Her father rushed in.

There is normally a space before a dash, as in the example above. However, if you are using it to interrupt a word, you may put the dash without a space before it. For example:

> You can't be seri— .

> He said, 'Please don't shoot me. Please d—.'

◑ Careful! 🖊

The single dash used to signal a break in thought or speech is informal. It is very useful to authors and journalists writing in the first person (that is using 'I', like a diary) because it gives an impression of immediacy. You see the interruption happening on the printed page. This use of the dash would be quite wrong in a considered report, because you want to give the impression that you have thought properly about all the issues before you started to write.

So think about what impression you want to give the reader before you use the single dash to signal a break in thought.

5. Hyphen

This is a hyphen (-).

What is the difference between a single dash and a hyphen? First of all, the hyphen is a very short line, and the dash is longer.

A dash separates off part of a sentence. There is always a space between a dash and each of the words separated by it. A hyphen, however, connects two parts of a word. It follows the last letter immediately, without a space between them. Except when it occurs at the end of a line, the next letter also follows it immediately without a space in between.

A hyphen can do several jobs: it can bring two words together to make a new one (called a compound word); it can also make clear the meaning and sound of a word, for example, *co-op* instead of *coop*.

(i) Using a hyphen in compound words:

Compound words are terms made up of two or more words. Sometimes the hyphen is essential. The following words, for example, appear with hyphens in all dictionaries.

> twenty-one
> mother-in-law

Some common prefixes (short additions to the front of a word) take a hyphen, such as *pre-, anti-, ex-, mid-, self-, quasi-*

> pre-contract
> anti-nuclear
> ex-husband
> mid-century
> self-conscious
> quasi-official

(ii) Using a hyphen to help pronounce a word:

> co-operation
> semi-inflated

(iii) Using a hyphen to separate letters so the meaning is clear:

> His pet project was the re-creation of Old London Bridge in California.

Here the word *re-creation* means 'creating again'. The hyphen makes it plain that you do not mean 'recreation', in the sense of relaxing and having fun.

(iv) Using a hyphen to join words that describe something:

There are some words you can join together, such as *old fashioned,* which together make a new meaning. When they come before the thing they describe, they are joined with a hyphen.

✐ EXAMPLES

Arabella longed for a fairy-tale wedding to Neil.

Mrs Findlay told Peaches that she prided herself on her old-fashioned taste. The Whole Nut Café's up-to-date décor did not appeal to her.

Here the describing words come before the thing they describe.

●⁑ Careful!

If the describing words come after the thing they describe or are used on their own, you do not join them with a hyphen.

✐ EXAMPLES

Neil suspected that marriage to Arabella would be more nightmare than fairy tale.

Peaches laughed and said that everything old fashioned was once up to date.

❤

The hyphen is also a matter of taste or house style. You will sometimes find words hyphenated in one dictionary but not in others. It is important to make sure that you find out what the house style is and stick to it. Be consistent. Remember that the aim of punctuation is to make things clear. Use a hyphen if you think it will help your reader to grasp your meaning.

✐ EXAMPLES

All the examples below are acceptable:

master-stroke	master stroke	masterstroke
take away	take-away	
love-life	love life	
commander-in-chief	commander in chief	

6. Ellipsis (horizontal dots)

Dots (...) are used to show:
— an idea or speech trailing off, *or*
— when some words are missing.

(i) Dots to show an idea or speech trailing off:

The general pointed out that the prisoner had five hours to decide whether to co-operate; after that ...

The intruders had left chaos: tumbled furniture,
ripped cushions, broken glass, blood ... oh no,
blood ...

Note: Remember to leave a space before and after the
dots.

Both these above examples expect the reader to put in
emotions, which are not spelled out. For that reason,
using an ellipsis can be helpful to writers of fiction or
anyone else wanting to raise the reader's temperature.
Use sparingly though. Readers don't like to be manipu-
lated too obviously.

(ii) Dots to show something missing:

Even people who have never read Rudyard
Kipling's 'If' know that the theme of the poem
is 'If you can keep your head when all about are
losing theirs ... you'll be a man, my son'.

An ellipsis in the middle of a quotation shows you are
leaving out something because:
— you are assuming the reader already knows it; *or*
— the missing words do not change the overall meaning.

7. Bullet points

Bullet points are used in reports, bids for contracts, memos, letters and presentations. They are used to create a list that is short and punchy. They appear a lot in Powerpoint presentations and other visual material. They are a good way of getting the attention of people who skim read, like many busy executives. They should be used sparingly, as they tire the eye.

Generally, bullet points follow an explanatory phrase with a colon (:). After that each point is indented and starts with a bullet mark. Your word processing package will have a bullet point facility which will indent for you automatically.

Individual bullet points often begin with a capital letter, especially when they are short. Most word processing packages do this for you automatically. Think of them as headings. On the other hand, some institutions prefer bullet points to start with a letter in the lower case. As always, consult the house style, and be consistent.

Short bullet points don't need punctuating (except for apostrophes, of course). Indeed, if your bullet point is long enough to need punctuation in order to make sense, then it is probably too long.

A bulleted list can feel incomplete, so it is usually a good idea to conclude with a sentence which puts the list in context. This should be set back against the margin.

(i) A list to grab the attention:

Before advertising this year's Beltane Feast, the
Dragon Council is respectfully requested to decide on:

- Start time
- Order of ceremonies
- Catering
- Cost of tickets
- Box Office Manager

Matilda will incorporate these details in the copy
she sends to the printer.

(ii) A list to summarize important points:

Another use of bullet points is to pull out important messages from a mass of material which follows.

Stewards are reminded that, in previous Beltane
Feasts, many problems could have been avoided by:

- supervising individual fires
- detecting disoriented dragonlets early in the
  festivities
- patrolling the perimeter of the Feast Ground
  regularly.

Grimbald's report on last year's experience follows, setting out in detail the preventive action he
recommends.

Some recommendations:

Organizations which use bullet points regularly in their
reports and presentations will have their own house
style. Some points which you may find helpful, however, are:

— Don't have more than five or six bullet points.
— Keep individual items short.
— Phrase your points consistently. For example, if you start off with *supervising,* make sure each successive point is set out as *-ing.*
— Organize your points. Put the most important first. Alternatively, start off with the first to happen chronologically.

Chapter Six

Speech Marks and Dialogue

This chapter covers how to punctuate speech and conversation, that is, when people talk. Speech marks are used in creative writing — novels, short stories, and so on — as well as in more factual writing, such as memoirs, biographies, and newspaper or magazine articles.

In this chapter we cover:
1. Using inverted commas for direct speech
2. Extended conversation
3. Indirect or reported speech

Inverted commas can be single or double. They look like this: single (' ') or double (" ").

1. Using inverted commas for direct speech

If you want to show what someone actually says or said, you enclose their words in inverted commas. This is called direct speech.

(i) Where to put the inverted commas, which in the UK are usually single:

✐ EXAMPLE

'We have a reporter coming to do an article on the Whole Nut Café on Tuesday.'

Note: There is always some form of punctuation immediately before you close inverted commas. It is normally a full stop or comma; occasionally it is a question mark, an exclamation mark or a dash.

Normal American usage for direct speech is double inverted commas, as in: "None of your business." You will find that older books printed in the UK also used the double form.

Either is fine, as long as you are consistent. If you are presenting a typescript to a particular publisher, find out their preferred style.

(ii) Where to put the inverted commas when the speaker says more than one sentence:

✍ EXAMPLE

'What time did the reporter from the Gazette say he'd be here, Neil? A motorbike has just drawn up. Wow, what a hunk!'

Note:
— you don't close the inverted commas until a person has finished speaking;
— the final exclamation mark goes inside the inverted commas.

Quiz 14

Saying more than one sentence at a time

Put inverted commas in the right place.

Tales of the Whole Nut Café

1. The reporter's called Isobel Cameron. That's obviously not her. Look at him, what a scruff!
2. Come on, Neil! He's a biker, that's all.
3. You're too tolerant, Peaches. He can't come in here if he's wearing a helmet.
4. Honestly, you sound just like your mother sometimes. Anyway, he's taking off his helmet.
5. Miranda's gone all pink! Are you OK?
6. He's coming in! Where's my comb? My hair's a mess!

(Answers on page 189)

(iii) Showing who is speaking:

There are two main ways to do this: with the speaker at the beginning or at the end. We give examples of both to show the punctuation.

✐ EXAMPLES

Sundeep said, 'Just look at that bike!'

Note:

— the first spoken word takes a capital letter, even though it follows a comma;
— there is a comma after said because it comes immediately before Sundeep's actual words, which are

shown by opening the inverted commas:

'I've lost my make-up bag,' squawked Miranda, in a tizzy.

— from the point of view of punctuation, *'I've lost my make-up bag,' squawked Miranda, in a tizzy* is only one sentence. That is why there is a comma, not a full stop, after *bag;*
— it also explains why there is a small *s* in *squawked* and not a capital letter.

Quiz 15

Punctuating conversation

Put in inverted commas, full stops, commas, question marks and capital letters where necessary.

1. Ranulf Forktail said I am sorry to report that the negotiations with the eagles have broken down
2. The eagles always were troublesome sighed Ermintrude
3. We can fight them put in Albreda's young nephew eagerly
4. Albreda looked at him and replied sternly there'll be no fighting, young dragon
5. The she-eagles don't want a war agreed Matilda
6. Grimbald nodded and added it's their egg-laying season they'll be fearful for their eggs
7. What about sending Matilda to talk to them suggested Albreda
8. What good would that do she'd only lecture them on she-eagles' rights snorted Ranulf, flicking his wings irritably

9. Ermintrude looked at him for a long moment and then said quietly just because you don't get on with her doesn't mean that she's not a good negotiator what's more she knows the she-eagles I second Albreda's suggestion

10. Athelstan Silverwing rose, swished his tail a few times, and declared Ermintrude's right the she-eagles may be willing to talk to Matilda it's worth a try

(Answers on page 189)

(iv) Showing who is speaking when breaking up speech:

Occasionally it is useful to name the speaker in the middle of what they say. Punctuation varies.

✎ EXAMPLES

'I hope you remembered to bring the onions,' Peaches said. 'We need them to start making the quiche.'

Note:

The speaker is named at the end of the first sentence, which we have already covered. You then need to open inverted commas again for her next sentence.

'If I bring the van round to the back of the café,' said Neil, looking harassed, 'young Sundeep can come and help me unload the vegetables.'

Note:

What does Neil actually say? He says, *'If I bring the van round to the back of the café, young Sundeep can come and help me unload the vegetables.'* This is only one sentence, although the writer has broken it up by putting, *said Neil, looking harassed* in the middle of it.

81

There are commas after *café* and *harassed* because the sentence isn't finished; and *said* and *young* do not begin with capital letters for the same reason.

Quiz 16

Showing who is speaking when breaking up speech

Put in inverted commas, capital letters, question marks, commas and full stops.

Tales of the Whole Nut Café

1. I'm really worried that Sundeep has had an accident said Peaches even he isn't usually two hours late.
2. What you mean retorted Miranda is that he's never been this late before
3. Don't think you need to worry Neil agreed he's probably overslept
4. Hi said Sundeep astonished to see them all standing around the café at this time in the morning did I miss something
5. I suppose drawled Miranda looking at the clock it's nice to know you're not dead
6. Dead Sundeep echoed, puzzled why should I be dead
7. When you didn't call pointed out Neil, trying not to laugh Peaches thought you'd fallen under a lorry
8. The least you could do said Miranda is make up a decent excuse
9. From now on Peaches told Sundeep you're here at nine o'clock on the dot or you get your cards
10. But Peaches whined Sundeep that's so unfair

(Answers on page 190)

Newspaper Style

When journalists wish to quote a whole sentence spoken by someone, they normally use the name of the speaker followed by a colon, rather than a comma, before the inverted commas. In this case, the inverted commas are double.

✐ EXAMPLE

Mr Findlay said: "The Whole Nut Café is an exciting new venture for all of us."

(v) Showing more than one person speaking:

When more than one person is speaking, this is called *dialogue*. Every time the speaker changes you need a new line. It should be indented.

✐ EXAMPLE

Arabella rushed to the café door and said, 'Oh Neil, I've been waiting for you.'

'Why? You shouldn't have bothered,' said Neil.

'Why not?' asked Arabella.

Note:

— you indent the first word the same number of spaces as for a new paragraph. (See section on paragraphs in Chapter 11.)

— the question mark here is followed by *asked* with a small *a*. You would do the same thing with an exclamation mark or the more usual comma.

— if you address somebody, you always need a comma to mark off their name, in this case *Neil*.

💣 Careful!

'You shouldn't have bothered.' Said Neil. ✗

This is wrong. Although *You shouldn't have bothered* could in theory be a complete sentence (that is, it could stand on its own), *Said Neil* is not a sentence. As we have said before, it might help you to think of the whole thing as one sentence. You need to use a comma to close the direct speech, as shown below.

'You shouldn't have bothered,' said Neil. ✔

☠ Mistakes People Make: talking to someone

If your character is talking to somebody, and uses his or her name or title, you really must mark it off with a comma. Otherwise, you can change the meaning entirely.

Having no success with *Love and Lucasta's Lord* at the moment, Belinda Bubblewit has tried her hand at a supernatural archaeological thriller, *Diana in the Dessert*. (We think she probably means 'Desert'.) The hero is supposed to be a kind of Indiana Jones. Alas, Belinda's writing style has not improved.

The night was silent. Diana crept round the sand dune after the robed figure. The tall mysterious figure had to be Professor de Wilde. He was searching among the tomb relics.

She could bear it no longer. She dashed out of hiding and grabbed his arm.

'Don't disturb them. You'll wake the dead professor.[1]'

He dropped the flash light.

'You made me jump Diana,[2]' he said. 'Over the years, sand must have covered the entrance to the Caves of Isis. Look for any sign of rock.'

Their eyes met in the darkness. He reached for her. Just then, there was a terrible roar and a ghostly phantom appeared.

'I am the goddess born again villain.[3] You have disturbed my rest.'

The shadow's fingers tightened round his throat. He plucked at them. Diana thought she might faint but watched in horror instead. The professor stretched out a writhing hand towards her. He seemed to be pointing.

'Diana rocks.[4]'

At the moment, it reads as though:

[1] Professor de Wilde will wake up a dead colleague

[2] he leaps over (or makes advances to) Diana

[3] either the goddess or the professor could be born again or a villain — or both!

[4] the professor takes time out of being strangled to flatter Diana or to point out her unsteadiness on her feet.

Diana in the Dessert has not found a publisher either.

Quiz 17

Setting out speech

Re-arrange the following with separate lines for each speaker and put in inverted commas where appropriate.

Tales of the Whole Nut Café

Peaches, did you see him? Who? The gorgeous hunk sitting by the window. The one who's got the earring and that sexy tattoo. For heaven's sake, Miranda, he looked as if he hadn't washed for a week and had just got out of bed. I wouldn't mind getting him back into bed, then. He's scrumptious. Honestly, girl, you're hopeless.

(Answers on page 190)

2. Extended conversation

Using inverted commas in speech paragraphs

As we saw above, you start a new line and indent every time a new person speaks. This convention will help you to identify who is speaking, so you do not have to keep on saying things like *Sundeep said, I remarked,* and so on.

Let's start by looking at a simple example:

> 'Why do you always start a seduction by offering a woman a glass of wine, Casanova?' I asked.
> 'My dear young man! I do not,' he said.
> 'Yes, you do. I've heard you often enough.'
> 'You must be mistaken.'

You might, however, want to add something which one of the speakers does either before or after he speaks. Where do you put it? You put it on the same line as his own words.

✐ EXAMPLE

> He frowned. 'You must be mistaken.'
>
> I listed them on my fingers. 'The Countess, Elisabetta, Caterina ... . And that is just this week.' I had a suspicion that he had even tried it with my sister but I was not going to bring that up now.
>
> His frown lifted. 'Ah. This week. That explains it. It is winter.' He patted me on the shoulder indulgently. 'Venice is much too cold in winter to ask a lady to come with me to take a sorbet.'

At some point, you will want to put in a new element of the story which does not naturally belong with any speech. When you do, it will need to be a new paragraph, starting on another line. Think of the writer as another speaker, if you like.

✐ EXAMPLE

> 'But why must it always be wine — or a sorbet?'
>
> Before he could answer, the door opened and his manservant brought in a letter on a silver tray. Casanova took it with a slight smile, as if to say that this was yet another assignation, and cast it aside, unread.
>
> The manservant withdrew.
>
> Casanova walked about the room for a few minutes, his hands clasped behind his back. The skirts

of his brocade coat swung as he turned, and the ruby on his left hand glinted in the firelight.

At last, he said in a thoughtful voice, 'I introduce to them this idea of a taste of delight which may also be a little naughty. A small indulgence, if you will. A minor excess which is always delicious.'

By the way, you will see that in the example above that Casanova does not always speak in sentences. Many of his remarks are just phrases. This is very much how we talk in our daily lives, unless we are making planned speeches.

However, sometimes a writer will want a character to continue at length. In order to avoid having a great block of text, the writer may decide to break up that speech into paragraphs, whilst his character is still talking. See the example below.

Note:
— you do not close the inverted commas until the speaker has finished speaking, however many paragraphs that takes;
— you must, however, put an inverted comma at the start of each new paragraph in the speech, just to remind your readers that he is still talking.

✐ EXAMPLE

'The secret of all seduction,' said Casanova, 'is to advance by degrees. You should offer — always offer, my dear sir, never enforce — you should offer to lead a lady one single step at a time.

'Nothing too dangerous at first. A small step from which she can retreat at any moment. And, to be honest, so can you, if the need arises.

'She may understand the moves of the game at once. Many do, like the Countess you speak of. On the other hand, like little Amalia, it may take her several meetings to see beyond the food and drink to — how shall I put it? — other possibilities.

'It is very like a dance. Two steps forward, one step back. Sometimes you lead and sometimes you only think you are leading. For, be very clear, my young friend, many ladies are far, far more skilled at the dance of seduction than you will ever be.'

● Careful!

Inverted commas are speech marks. They indicate that someone is saying something aloud. You do not use them to show thoughts.

You do not use inverted commas to show direct speech if you are writing a play or a script for film, radio or television. There are conventions on how to set out such work so that actors can follow them and directors and technical staff can add their own requirements. You need to research whatever applies to your particular form before you submit a script.

3. Indirect speech: reporting what somebody else has said

There are two ways of showing what somebody says. The first is direct speech, using speech marks, as we have shown already:

'You have travelled to some wonderful cities, Casanova. I envy you Paris and St Petersburg especially.'

'Ah, but people are the same in every city, Signora Leon,' said Casanova, 'and nowhere is as beautiful as Venice.'

The second is indirect or reported speech, for example:

Signora Leon said that Casanova had travelled to some wonderful cities. She envied him Paris and St Petersburg especially.

Casanova said that people were the same in every city and nowhere was as beautiful as Venice.

Quiz 18

Turning direct speech into indirect or reported speech

The following are direct statements, either spoken aloud or thought. Turn them into the indirect form, as set out in the examples above, removing inverted commas where necessary.

1. 'I, Ermintrude Glop, was once known as the belle of Glen Tuath.'
2. 'I was famous for my beautifully pointed ears and shining scales.'
3. 'Athelstan Silverwing's ode to the loveliness of my ears won the poetry competition at the winter festival.'
4. Rollo Silverwing thought, look at old Ermintrude flaring her nostrils at Grandfather. It's gross.
5. Yes, you were once beautiful, thought Athelstan, but now you talk too much.

(Answers on page 191)

Quiz 19

Turning indirect speech or thoughts into direct speech or thoughts

As set out in the examples on page 90, recast these sentences, adding inverted commas where necessary to turn the sentence into direct speech or thought. Remember that you do not use inverted commas for thoughts.

1. Matilda said that dragons came from far and near to sample Albreda's word beer.
2. Albreda was worried that she'd forgotten to put in a teaspoonful of fly agaric mushroom which made all the difference.
3. Her mother always complained that she made it too strong.

4. Rolló said that she never made enough.
5. Grimbald complimented Albreda that this year's was a fine vintage and one of her best.

(Answers on page 191)

For direct and indirect questions, see Chapter 7 (pages 93–97).

For quotations within direct and indirect speech, see Chapter 10 (pages 124–36).

Question Marks

In this chapter we cover:
1. What a question mark does
2. Direct questions
3. Indirect questions
4. Mid-sentence question mark
5. Showing doubt

1. What a question mark does

This is a question mark (?).

A question mark is used to do two things:
— to signal that the writer wants something answered
— to show doubt

2. Direct questions

A direct question is where we see the question exactly as it was asked. The question mark follows the question. This is usually, but not always, at the end of a sentence.

✐ EXAMPLES

Am I going to be late?
Do you agree?
'Does he care?' I asked.
Was there ever a problem which Superman could not solve?
Who is the man in black?
Where is the exit?

Why did they run away?

When will the police arrive?

How on earth did you reach that conclusion?

'Will you take a glass of wine, my lady?' asked
Casanova.

3. Indirect questions

An indirect question is one that is reported by somebody
else. It does not take a question mark.

✐ EXAMPLES

Casanova asked the lady if she would
take a glass of wine.

Here Casanova is not asking the question
directly. The writer is telling us what he did, so
there is no question mark. If you want to turn
this into a direct question, you might have:

'Will you take a glass of wine, my
lady?' purred Casanova.

Similarly:
Elisabetta wondered whether her
mother would disapprove if she
accepted a glass of wine from this
charming stranger.

Here Elisabetta is thinking her argument
through to herself. If you want to turn this
into a direct question, you might say:

Elisabetta was in a quandary. Surely Mamma
would not think that there was any harm in
accepting a glass of wine from this charming
stranger?

Quiz 20

Direct or indirect question?

Decide whether these are direct or indirect questions and
put in a full stop or a question mark, as necessary.

Dragon Deeds

1. I, Norbert, am the handsomest, most golden dragon on
   the mountain. Why does nobody love me
2. Who told you that you were the handsomest dragon,
   Norbert
3. Grimbald thought, when would Norbert learn not to
   be so boastful
4. As the two dragons glared at each other, Albreda
   arrived and asked what was the matter
5. Where is Ermintrude Is she still in the wild wood
   communing with the dragon ancestors
6. Will Ermintrude be back when the moon has risen
   over the mountain lake
7. When does the moon rise over the mountain lake
8. Why is it that when Ermintrude is mysterious I am
   rather frightened but when Matilda is, I only want to
   laugh
9. Why it is that Ermintrude is such powerful figure
   among the dragons, I have not the slightest idea

10. Grimbald wondered why Ranulf Forktail was such an old windbag Was it because his father had not listened to him when he was young

(Answers on page 191)

Quiz 21

Turning direct questions into indirect questions

✐ EXAMPLE

Neil said, 'Sundeep, can you stop that man by the window making those odd noises?'

As an indirect question, this would be:

Neil asked Sundeep if he could stop the man by the window making odd noises.

Turn the following into indirect questions:

Tales of the Whole Nut Café

1. 'Are you going to be sick?' asked Sundeep, looking at the customer's green face.
2. 'Where's the Gents?' groaned the customer.
3. 'Hey, did you put laburnum seeds in that cake, after all?' Sundeep called out to Miranda.
4. 'Don't be stupid,' said Miranda. 'Would I really do a thing like that?'
5. Why did Sundeep always get hold of the wrong end of the stick?

(Answers on page 192)

Quiz 22

Turning indirect questions into direct questions

✐ EXAMPLE

Neil wondered what was wrong with laburnum.

As a direct question, this would be:

'What's wrong with laburnum?' asked Neil.

Turn the following into direct questions (how people would say them aloud):

Tales of the Whole Nut Café

1. The lady in the corner said that surely laburnum was poisonous.
2. Sundeep said gleefully that it certainly was and suggested that they wait and see if the customer turned green.
3. The lady in the corner pushed her coffee away abruptly while her companion asked whether Sundeep was serious.
4. Miranda fled to the kitchen and a moment later Peaches stormed out demanding what the matter was.
5. Peaches assured the ladies in the corner that no part of the laburnum was allowed inside the Whole Nut Café and asked whether they would like a complimentary cup of coffee.

(Answers on page 192)

4. Mid-sentence question mark

Can a direct question come in the middle of a sentence, not at the end? If so, where do I put the question mark?

The most common use is probably in reported speech. Other mid-sentence question marks tend to confuse readers, so be careful.

✐ EXAMPLE

> Three of them — but why did they run
> away? — were never heard of again.

Here the question is a strong idea inserted in mid-sentence, and separated by double dashes.

It is also possible to have a mid-sentence question mark which belongs in a quotation or title.

✐ EXAMPLE

> At first I thought of taking her to see *Who's Afraid of Virgina Woolf?* but then I decided it was not the right play for a girls' jolly evening out.

Remember that the point of punctuation is to help the reader understand. Readers usually expect a question mark to come at the end. Our strong advice is to avoid a mid-sentence question mark if possible.

For formal writing, such as business or academic reports, contracts, official or business letters you should never have a mid-sentence question mark, except in the specific case of a question mark in brackets, see below under 'Showing doubt'. Otherwise, it will look as if you haven't taken time to think properly about what you wanted to say.

MID-SENTENCE QUESTION MARKS

Creative writers, in particular, might want to suggest a particular state of mind in one of their characters and the mid-sentence question mark could well do this. It can suggest that the character is not very sophisticated or well educated; or that he/she is hurried and confused, even desperate.

✐ EXAMPLE

I did not know which way to turn, right? left? into the mist? away from it? And my heart banged like that monster engine behind me.

If you do choose to do this, do it sparingly. It can hurry and confuse your reader too!

5. Showing doubt

A question mark in brackets can be used to show doubt anywhere in a sentence.

✐ EXAMPLES

Daniel was born in 1897 (?) and his first hit was *On the Strut.*

This means that the year of Daniel's birth is unconfirmed, though probable.

The train we need to catch for Oxford leaves
Paddington (Platform 9?) at 9.20am.

This means that the writer is helpfully suggesting a
platform number but is not absolutely certain, whereas
he/she is certain about the time of the train.

She will be doing a book tour of the United States
in September, taking in all the major east coast
cities and various other centres (Kansas City?
Dubuque? Raleigh, North Carolina?) which we
will inform you of at a later date.

This probably means that the named venues have not
yet been confirmed. (Local TV in Raleigh, Durham, no
dinner and the last flight onwards to the next destination.
We feel for her!)

Chapter Eight

Exclamation Marks, Italics, Bold and Underlining

In this chapter we cover:
1. Exclamation marks
2. Italics
3. Bold
4. Underlining

1. Exclamation marks

This is an exclamation mark (!).

An exclamation mark is used for emphasis. By using it the writer wants to show:

— a command *or*
— a warning *or*
— a sense of urgency *or*
— very strong emotion *or*
— surprise *or*
— scepticism

Normally, it comes at the end of a short sharp word or phrase which is, as it says, an exclamation. It may also come at the end of a longer sentence or phrase instead of a full stop.

✎ EXAMPLES

— Command:
> Come here!
> Pick those feet up!
> Remember, you are unique!

— Warning:

> Look out!
> Fire!
> Behind you!

— Very strong emotion:

> I hate you!
> Oh, bliss!
> What an amazing profile I have!

— Surprise:

> That is a ludicrous suggestion!
> She slipped past the minders and asked the Prince to dance!
> He crossed the Gobi desert alone!

— Scepticism (doubt):

> According to Caterina, Casanova offered to give up every other woman for her sake!
> According to Casanova, Caterina never told the truth!

— Emphasis:

> We feel for her! (as we used it on page 100)

Occasionally you see an exclamation mark in brackets, sometimes without any words at all, to indicate surprise and scepticism (see Chapter 5, pages 64–65).

The exclamation mark is often used at the end of a sentence of direct speech. In that case, the exclamation mark replaces the final comma or full stop and comes *inside* the inverted commas.

✐ EXAMPLE

'How extraordinary!' he gasped.

There are some people who will tell you that the exclamation mark should not be used at all in good writing. Their argument is that if you need to put an exclamation mark after something to show that you mean strong emotion, then you have not expressed yourself very well.

You may think this is making a mountain out of a molehill. After all, we see exclamation marks everywhere, particularly in personal emails and on internet chat boards. You can put an exclamation mark in a note to friends and, because they know you, they will have a pretty clear idea of whether you are ordering them to do something, being strongly emotional, surprised or ironic. But it is a lot more difficult when your reader does not know you. You might come across as opinionated, pushy or over-emotional.

So we would advise you to be careful with exclamation marks. It is best not to use them at all in any formal writing. If you do use exclamation marks, do it sparingly or else it will look as though you are either over-excited or a bit naïve. In particular, if you are given to several exclamation marks !!!! or any variation of ??!! to indicate surprise and disbelief. Keep them for your closest friends.

Writers of fiction may find exclamation marks useful, most usually in dialogue or comedy.

☠ Mistakes People Make: over-exclaiming!!

Belinda Bubblewit has sent several chapters of her Restoration novel, *Love and Lucasta's Lord,* to a publisher. Here is an extract:

> Lucasta fled down the darkened corridor, away from that Beast! That Barbarian, Sir Edwin Dastard!
>
> A door was flung open and she felt herself clasped in the muscular arms of none other than Lord Dragonmere!
>
> He was here! He had come to save her! Her heart pounded under the froth of lace and her bosom heaved!
>
> Lord Dragonmere's magnificent shoulders quivered! His smouldering black eyes flashed! His manly chest swelled!
>
> 'Miss Derby! ... Lucasta! ...' He fell to his knees, picked up the hem of her dainty robe and raised it to his lips!!
>
> 'Oh, my lord!' Lucasta could scarcely breathe!
>
> 'Lucasta, I love thee! Passionately! Madly! To Desperation! Wilt thou trust thyself to Me?!'
>
> Lucasta fainted!!

Alas, the publisher returned her manuscript without a word of encouragement.

2. Italics

What are italics? *This sentence is in italics.* If you were writing a note by hand and wanted to emphasize something, you would underline it. Basically, italics are the printed version of that handwritten underlining. When you are writing dialogue, a word in italics is one which the speaker really stresses.

Italics do mainly four things:
— emphasize something
— indicate foreign words or phrases
— indicate titles of complete works
— make a block of text stand out from the main body of the work

Italics for emphasis:

✐ EXAMPLES

Desert means a waterless waste and *desert* means to abandon.

'No, Signor Casanova,' said Donna Emilia firmly, 'You may *not* kiss me!'

'Help,' said the chambermaid in an extremely small voice. 'Oh, Signor Casanova, do not do that. Oh no. Oh dear. *Oh yes, please.*'

Italics to indicate foreign words or phrases:

✏ EXAMPLES

   a) Grimbald said that eagles were eagles and, *ipso facto,* dangerous.
   b) Matilda said that he was a pompous windbag, a show-off, too big for his boots, etc., etc. and could he speak English, *por favor?*
   c) 'We meet again, *chérie,'* said Casanova, with a flourish of his fine hat.
   d) Neil looked gorgeous in his kilt and black velvet jacket but Peaches was worried to see the dagger in his sock, though he insisted that it was a traditional *sgean dhu* and absolutely essential.

e) Remembering his mother's stern instructions, Neil turned to the French Ambassador's wife and said bravely, 'Would you care to dance, *madame?*'

💣 Careful!

You do not put foreign titles like Monsieur, Madame or Signor in italics, when they are part of a name, for example, Monsieur Chambertin, Madame Chanel, Signor Casanova. If you want to use them as a form of address, as in example (e) above, they normally go into italics.

Although italicizing foreign titles is correct, if you were writing an entire book about Casanova, or setting a novel in, say, France, italicizing every *Madame* or *Signor* would look clumsy and spoil the flow for the reader. Your editor might well decide to dispense with the italics. For this reason, we, too, have dispensed with italics for the Casanova sections in this book.

Many foreign words have entered our language, such as 'chic' (French), 'pyjamas' (Urdu) or 'kiosk' (Turkish). Originally, they were printed in italics. Over time, they have become naturalized, and the italics have been dropped. Originally, foreign phrases like etc., i.e. and e.g. were in italics. These days they are in standard print.

Italics for titles of complete works:

✎ EXAMPLES

> *The Magic Flute* (opera)
> *The Times* (newspaper)
> *A Room with a View* (novel)
> *Evita* (musical)
> *Cosmopolitan* (magazine)

Note that *The* and *A* are italicized if they are part of the title.

Exceptions: The Bible and the Koran are *not* italicized.

Italics for blocks of text:

You will often find that extracts from diaries or letters are in italics, to differentiate them from the main body of the text. You find this most commonly in novels, biographies and some books about history. In newspapers and magazines, advice columns usually print readers' letters in italics and the columnists' answers in standard print.

✎ EXAMPLE

> Carlo strode through the cobbled streets of Paris, bearing Casanova's note. He had, of course, prised open the seal and read it.

Signore

*Giacomo Casanova presents his compliments and
would be glad to receive the thousand louis which
he won from you at the Maison d'Or last month.
This is the second time he has made this request.
He is obliged to remind you that no gentleman
ignores his debts of honour.*

Carlo smiled to himself. He knew that if he came
to this house again, it would be to bring a chal-
lenge from his master, whose skill with the small
sword was second to none.

A final word of advice:

To sum up, in the words of the master: 'Italics should, in
good writing, be used with caution and in moderation;
their most legitimate purpose is to indicate emphasis
in dialogue, and everywhere else, to indicate foreign
words and phrases and titles.' (Eric Partridge, *Usage and
Abusage: a Guide to Good English*)

3. Bold

This sentence is in bold type. It is used to highlight
important information.

We have been asked what is the difference between italics
and bold. Italics tend to emphasize important words or
phrases within a body of text. By contrast, bold type covers the whole statement. Bold type either gives instructions
or announces that important information will follow.

In books, bold type is sometimes used for chapter headings, section headings or captions for graphs or illustrations etc. This means that you would be very unlikely to find bold type used in the body of a novel.

Bold type is most widely used in forms and official letters. You will often find the subject of a letter set out in bold, for example.

4. Underlining

A general rule is: don't!

However ...

In the past, some publishers preferred words or phrases to be underlined in the author's typescript which were intended to be in italic in the printed book. This is because it was easier for the typesetters to spot. This is changing, as most text is now transferred electronically.

Businesses, the public sector, colleges, universities, publishing houses etc. all have their own house style and conventions on presentation. We have given you some working principles but do make sure that you ask for the house style guide.

Your computer may automatically underline addresses on the world wide web, such as: casanova@heartthrobsrus. com or www.feminist-egg-laying.com

This automatic feature creates active hyperlinks in the text. If you are preparing a manuscript for publication, you should switch off all automatic coding, including this one. If you want to include a web address, you can insert the underlining manually.

Chapter Nine

Capital Letters, Titles and Abbreviations

In this chapter we cover:
1. Names and titles
2. Initials
3. Abbreviations
4. Capitals to make a literary point

The capital (upper case) letter is always larger than a standard (lower case) letter, and often looks different, for instance, *A* and *a*, *Q* and *q*.

We have already said in Chapter 1 that you use a capital letter at the start of a new sentence.

There are other words which always take a capital letter in English, even when they are in the middle of a sentence.

1. Names and titles

We use capitals for the names and titles of people, places and things.

Identifying yourself:

I — as in, *'Where am I?'* This is always capitalized wherever it comes in a sentence. Note that *you, he, she, we, they* are only capitalized at the start of a sentence.

Names of people, gods and fictional characters:

Casanova
Julia
Apollo
Hamlet

Titles of people:

These take capital letters when they go with a name:

Mr Mandela
Dame Kelly Holmes
Dr Fox
Sir David Attenborough

When titles refer to a particular person and there is no doubt who is intended, they take a capital.

— *the Queen,* meaning, for example, Elizabeth II, or the Queen of Hearts.

Compare: *Casanova made her feel like a queen.*

— *the Doctor,* meaning, for example, Dr Doolittle.

Compare: *Every ship has a doctor.*

— *the Head,* meaning, for example, Mr Squeers, Head of Dotheboys Hall.

Compare: *Being a teacher is only interesting if you can see yourself becoming head one day.*

Words for family relationships — mother, father, uncle, grandmother, and so on — take a capital letter *only* when they are a substitute for a name. If you want to test whether a word needs a capital letter, see if you can replace it with a given name and the sentence still makes sense.

I remember Mother warning me against men
like you.

but

Julia's mother told her to avoid men who offered
her a ride in a gondola.

Names of places:

Venice	Lake Como
Adriatic Sea	the Gobi Desert
River Danube	Kew Botanical Gardens
the Doge's Palace	the Deep South
Asia	

You only use capitals when you are referring to a specific place. You do not normally capitalize the points of
the compass (north, south, east and west) except when
they are part of a name of a location, for example:

The Mid West has always been suspicious of East
Coast intellectuals.

but

He took his ship down the east coast of the conti-
nent as far as he dared, landed in a natural harbour,
and struck out west the next day.

Nations, regions, languages, religious/ethnic groups:

Italy
Turkish palaces
the Balkans

> Casanova spoke Italian, French, Spanish and Latin
> a Buddhist priest
> the Polynesian people

A few national or regional words lose meaningful links with their origins as they become part of our own culture. In those cases it is *a matter of choice* whether the word takes a capital letter, for instance, alsatian (dog), french window, yorkshire pudding, bordeaux (wine).

However, in the case of the wonderful wine, champagne, you only give it a capital letter at the start of a sentence.

Planets and celestial bodies:

> Saturn
> Andromeda
> the Milky Way

You only capitalize 'earth', 'sun' and 'moon' when you are naming them as celestial bodies, for example:

> Venus, Mercury, Mars, Jupiter, Saturn, Uranus,
> Neptune, Pluto and the Earth all rotate round the
> Sun, while the Moon rotates about the Earth.

But compare:

> The population of the earth is growing unsustainably.

Sometimes poets and other writers may capitalize 'earth', 'sun' and 'moon' — see Section 3, page 120.

Days, months, festivals:

Monday
January
May Day
Christmas
Diwali
Ramadan
Yom Kippur

You do *not* capitalize the seasons, spring, summer, autumn (fall) or winter, although sometimes poets have done so (see Section 3, page 120).

*Titles of works of art, including
newspapers and periodicals:*

Only important words take capital letters, including the first word:

Star Trek
To Kill a Mockingbird
The Last Supper
A Nightingale Sang in Berkeley Square
The Times
Private Eye

Names of restaurants, cafés, pubs, clubs:

Important words take capital letters, including the first:

The King's Head
The Magpie and Stump
Stop 'n' Snack
The Nite Place

Note, however, that you do *not* have a capital 'T' in front of the name of hotels, such as the Savoy or the Ritz, unless it is at the start of a sentence.

Names of ships, vehicles and instruments:

> the Cutty Sark
> the Flying Scotsman
> Voyager 1
> the Hubble Space Telescope

Here, *Voyager* gets a capital letter because it is the name of the spacecraft. However, you refer to the 'Voyager programme' and the 'Voyager mission', without capitalizing the *second* word, unless it forms part of the title of an article or book, for example, 'The Voyager Programme Re-examined'.

Titles of academic courses:

> Microbiology
> Structural Analysis in Germany 1900–1920
> The Romantic Poets and their Friends

Brand names:

> Rolex
> Bollinger
> Maserati
> Villeroy & Boch

Some brand names have become so widely identified with the product that they don't take an initial capital letter any more: *a hoover, a magimix, a biro.*

Names of organizations:

United Nations
the Red Cross
National Aeronautics and Space Administration
Federal Bureau of Investigation
British Broadcasting Corporation

2. Initials

Capitals are used in the middle of sentences to indicate the names of organizations and publications which are well known — at least to the audience at whom a particular piece of writing is aimed. Capitals are also used for widely recognized concepts. Note that in uses like these, there are no spaces in between the capital letters.

Organizations:

the UN
NASA
the FBI
the BBC
the OECD (Organization for Economic Co-operation and Development)
IFIs (International Financial Institutions. Note that the 's' which makes the plural is in the *lower* case.)

Publications:

IFS   International Financial Statistics
BMJ   British Medical Journal
PMLA   Publications of the Modern Language Association

Concepts:

IQ (Intelligence Quotient)
Q&A (Question and Answer)
FAQs (Frequently Asked Questions. Note that the
  's' which makes the plural is in the lower case.)
R&R (Rest and Recreation, a military term
  originally)
ROM (Read-Only Memory)

3. Full stops after shortened words

A full stop can be used to show that a word has been shortened to the first few letters.

✐ EXAMPLES

Reverend shortened to *Rev.*
literary criticism shortened to *lit. crit.*
General shortened to *Gen.*
Captain shortened to *Capt.*

💣 Careful!

If you shorten a word by cutting out letters in the middle, there is no full stop.

✐ EXAMPLES

Mister shortened to *Mr*
Mistress shortened to *Mrs, Miss* or *Ms*
Doctor shortened to *Dr*

---

3. Capitals to make a literary point

There are no real rules governing literary or poetic usage, but there are many examples.

For instance, when Shelley wrote: *'O wild West Wind, thou breath of Autumn's being,'* he capitalized three words which we would normally expect to see in the lower case. This is because he is using 'West Wind' as a name and 'Autumn', perhaps, as a kind of god.

In Terry Pratchett's *Discworld* series of novels, his character Death speaks in capital letters throughout — that is every letter of every word is capital, not just the first letter. This does give the impression of an echoey other-worldliness to Death's dialogue, even when he is talking about quite ordinary things like chocolate. It is wearing on the eye, though. (Fortunately, Death tends not to speak in long sentences nor to stick around too long.)

Some authors use initial capitals in the middle of sentence to reflect a character's way of speaking and thinking, such as self-importance, pretension, and so on. P.G. Wodehouse, a master of the English language, as well as a great storyteller and a comic genius, uses this to good effect. For self-importance there is Lord Emsworth's keen-eyed secretary whom Wodehouse calls the Efficient Baxter. However, nobody beats Bertie Wooster for sheer pretension. In the following extract, his Aunt Dahlia asks Bertie if she may consult his valet, Jeeves, for advice on re-uniting her daughter Angela with Tuppy Glossop, the love of Angela's life, who has fallen for another girl . . .

'Jeeves's services will not be required,' I said. 'I can handle this business. The programme which I have laid out will be quite sufficient to take young Tuppy's mind off love-making. It is my intention to insert the Luminous Rabbit in his room at the first opportunity that presents itself. The Luminous Rabbit shines in the dark and jumps about, making odd squeaking noises. It will sound to young Tuppy like the Voice of Conscience, and I anticipate that a single treatment will make him retire into a nursing-home for a couple of weeks or so. At the end of which period, he will have forgotten all about the bally girl.'

'Bertie,' said Aunt Dahlia with a sort of frozen calm, 'you are the Abysmal Chump.'

(From 'The Ordeal of Young Tuppy', published in the short story collection *Very Good, Jeeves,* P.G. Wodehouse, 1930.)

Creative writers may want to capitalize the first letters of certain words in their *own* voice, not just when one of their characters is speaking. This stylistic device can deliver a number of different effects, depending on the context. Make sure that you do it in such a way that your reader will understand your intention.

Rudyard Kipling famously used 'Gentlemen', the old Sussex euphemism for 'smuggler' in his poem 'Smuggler's Song'. By capitalizing 'Gentlemen', in the same way as those respectable people the Parson and the Clerk, he adds a sinister power to the idea of these silent, secret people who must not be looked at.

Five and twenty ponies
Trotting through the dark —
Brandy for the Parson,
'Baccy for the Clerk;
Laces for a lady, letters for a spy,
And watch the wall, my darling, while
    the Gentlemen go by!

In a traditional layout, as here, most poems take capital letters at the beginning of each line, even though it may not be the beginning of a sentence. This may not be the case with modern poetry. Indeed, some modern poetry has no capitals at all.

☠ Mistakes People Make: over-capitalization

Belinda Bubblewit, who wants to write an historical novel and can't understand why publishers keep rejecting *Love and Lucasta's Lord,* starts every word which she thinks is important with a capital letter:

> Sir Edwin Dastard threw Lucasta over his Shoulder and uttered a Foul Expletive.
>
> 'Unhand me, Sir,' she cried. 'Whither art thou taking Me?'
>
> 'To my Ship,' he replied with an evil Leer.
>
> At that moment, the Dowager Countess leaped in through the Window from the Balcony and cried, 'Halt, Villain! Unhand my Niece.'
>
> 'Nay, Madam, you jest,' retorted the wicked Sir Edwin. 'No one can Stop Me. Once aboard the Lugger and the Wench is Mine!'

Chapter Ten

Inverted Commas
for Quotations and Titles

In this chapter we cover:
1. Quotations in articles, reports or essays
2. Titles using inverted commas
3. Quotes within quotes
4. The ironic 'so-called' use

As we saw in Chapter 6, inverted commas are used as speech marks. They can also be used as quotation marks or to mark out titles of articles, poems, musical works or paintings.

1. Quotations in articles, reports or essays

Quotation marks are used to mark off what somebody other than the writer has either said or written (see also Chapter 6, page 77).

They look like this: double quotation marks (" "), single quotation marks (' ')

✐ EXAMPLES

The following examples are all extracts from Matilda Hurstpank's *Egg-laying is a Feminist Issue:*

A short quotation of a few words:

> Research has shown that female dragons who pro-
> duce more than two clutches of eggs a year have,
> as Ermintrude Glop argues, 'problems with regain-
> ing their flight muscles'. They feel that they have
> 'lost status' because they cannot fly far.

You will see that:

— there is a comma before the first quotation opens.
  This is because it is indirect speech (see page 90)
  which quotes Ermintrude's actual words;
— the 'p' of *problems* does not take a capital letter. This
  is because Matilda Hurstpank has used only a short
  phrase and so the quotation is treated as part of the
  sentence;
— the quotation mark at the end of the first quotation,
  'problems with regaining their flight muscles', comes
  before the full stop. This is an important difference
  from direct speech, where the final punctuation always comes inside the inverted commas;
— Matilda does not have to repeat that the second quotation is also from Ermintrude Glop because the two
  are so close together.

American style is different. If a sentence ends with
a quote, the punctuation ending the sentence must
come inside the speech marks.

> Research has shown that female dragons who
> produce more than two clutches of eggs a year
> have, as Ermintrude Glop argues, "problems with
> regaining their flight muscles."

A quotation of a complete sentence:

> Research has shown that female dragons who produce more than two clutches of eggs a year feel that they have lost status by being unable to undertake long flights. When I spoke to the venerable Ermintrude Glop, she told me, 'They have problems with regaining their flight muscles and their mobility is much reduced.'

You will see that:
— there is a comma before the quotation opens;
— what Ermintrude says is a complete sentence. Therefore, it starts with a capital letter;
— the final full stop comes *before* the last quotation mark. This is because what Ermintrude says is a complete sentence, rather than just a phrase.

Longer quotations:

> The effect of too much egg-laying on the morale of female dragons cannot be underestimated. Adeliza Redwald's testimony may prove my point:

> > That year I laid three clutches of eggs. It was awful. I felt ungainly and heavy the whole time. The moment I'd raised one clutch I was back at the beginning and laying another. By the end of the third clutch, I was exhausted. (Adeliza Redwald, *Out of the Nest,* Draca Press 2005, p.25.)

> It is clear that this female dragon is in bondage both to her reproductive system and to a society which

expects young female dragons to want nothing more
out of life than to lay eggs and raise young dragons.

You will see that:
— longer quotations usually have their own paragraph
   (see Chapter 11, page 137);
— the quotation is preceded by a colon;
— the whole quotation is indented at the left margin;
— when laid out like this, the quotation does not need to
   be in quotation marks as well.

Note:
A longer quotation is defined by some organizations as
having more than two lines. Others say more than four.
Some house styles will use italics, some a smaller type
size, some just indenting.

What we set out here are the basic conventions. Individual
organizations, universities, businesses and publications
will have their own preferred style. So it is important to
check before you submit a piece of commissioned work.

Referencing:

If you are using quotations from other sources, it is important to tell your reader where to look up the original. This is called *referencing*.

In the example above, you will see that we have shown the book from which the writer is quoting, in this way: (Adeliza Redwald, *Out of the Nest,* Draca Press 2005, p.25.) This gives all the information you need (in this case, author, title, publisher, date, page number) to find the quotation in the original book. Or, you can reference briefly, e.g. Redwald 2005, p.25, and explain more fully in the bibliography at the end of the book. The bibliography sets out full details of all the books and articles you have consulted.

There are a number of different ways to reference. It is important to comply with the house style.

Quiz 23

Quotations in the body of a text

Insert the following quotations correctly in the text below.

Quotation 1
one clutch of eggs should be quite enough for any female dragon, given that each clutch contains between four to eight eggs. Let her spread her wings a little first, find out what life is all about before she settles down to lay eggs. She will be a much better mother for having some experience of life.

Quotation 2
the right to choose

Quotation 3
should be allowed to develop other skills

Quotation 4
My proudest moment came when I was awarded the gold medal for egg-laying.

Quotation 5
female dragons' rights

Dragon Deeds

From: *The Importance of Egg-Laying* by Grimbald Fire-Plume

I repeat, the whole future of the dragon race is at stake and we cannot allow the decline in egg-laying to continue. The blame for this state of affairs undoubtedly lies at the door of Matilda Hurstpank, whose *Egg-Laying is a Feminist Issue* has reached the bestseller lists. I cannot believe that any sensible dragon will be taken in for a moment by Hurstpank's argument that *[quotation 1]*

It is a she-dragon's duty to egg-lay, it is what she is born to do and this modern notion of she-dragons having, as Ermintrude Glop says *[quotation 2]* is dangerous nonsense.

Mrs Glop's view is that she-dragons *[quotation 3]*

What greater role in life could any she-dragon have than bringing young dragons into the world? My own grandmother laid twenty-one clutches of eggs and declared *[quotation 4]*

She is the true example to all young she-dragons, not the madness of Miss Hurstpank.

I am confident that this idea of so-called *[quotation 5]*

will be seen for the false argument it is. Only ugly she-dragons will follow Miss Hurstpank; truly feminine she-dragons will scorn such ways of gaining attention and do what they do best: lay eggs and safeguard the future of the dragon race.

(Answers on page 193)

2. Single inverted commas to show a title

Traditionally, titles of all artistic works (books, plays, operas, paintings, music, and so on) took inverted commas. You can still use inverted commas if you are writing by hand or using an email programme which does not have an italics facility.

Nowadays, the titles of complete or extensive works of art or periodicals go into italics as we set out in Chapter 8, page 108. Only titles of short pieces of writing or music, for instance, a poem, a song, a CD, or a newspaper or magazine article, take inverted commas.

✎ EXAMPLES

> Neil and Peaches rolled home from the party hand in hand, singing all the words they could remember of 'All You Need is Love' at the tops of their voices.

As soon as he got home, Neil sent Peaches a copy of a poem called 'There is a Lady Sweet and Kind'.

At coffee the next morning, Neil was too embarrassed to look at Peaches and buried his head in an article in *The Times* called 'Small businesses: the first five years'.

Note:
— the inverted commas are like a picture frame which encloses the title. So, in the second and third examples above, the final full stop is after the second (closing) inverted comma.
— most titles of songs and poems use capital letters for the important words.
— in quoting the titles of newspaper articles, you should follow the punctuation of the original. *The Times,* for example, gives a capital letter to the first word only.

●⃰ Careful!

Some points to watch out for:
— In business and academic work, the convention is that if you quote a work in your paper, for example, Egg-laying is a Feminist Issue by Matilda Hurstpank, you underline the title instead of using inverted commas or italics. Different organizations have their own preferred house style, however, and you should check with them. Whichever style you use, you should always be consistent.

> — Names of houses, estates, buildings and jobs do not take inverted commas unless you want to suggest that the titles are in some sense unreal or undeserved — see (4) the 'so-called' use, page 135.
> — Names of styles of music or art don't take inverted commas, although sometimes they take capital letters, for example Motown, Cubism.

Quiz 24

Showing titles

Some of the titles in this quiz need italics, some need inverted commas, some need no change. Show which is needed. Be careful, they may not always be necessary.

Tales of the Whole Nut Café

1. Miranda was reading Daphne Flowerdew's latest book, The Karma of Herbs.
2. Sundeep's homework was to read the article Spreadsheets for Individuals this week and Spreadsheets for Business by the end of term.
3. Sundeep was convinced that Biker's Blues was the best movie ever.
4. Neil asked Peaches to go with him to the organic food seminar at Hoddletone Hall.
5. The first session was called Whole Food or Horrible Food?
6. All through coffee, the sound system played Strawberry Fair over and over again.

7. The sound system was clearly broken, so Neil made them call Events Noise Ltd, the suppliers.
8. Miranda was proud of her new title, Acting Manager, even though it was only for two days.
9. Neil told Peaches that his two favourite operas were Don Giovanni and Tosca.
10. He told Peaches wistfully that in Don Giovanni every woman on the stage falls in love with Don Giovanni at some point during the opera.

(Answers on page 194)

3. Quotes within quotes

The most common example of quotes within quotes occurs when you use quotation marks in the middle of when someone is speaking.

> Miranda said, 'Neil, have you read this article, "Planting tomatoes by moonlight", in *The Green-Fingered Gardener*?'

Here, the British convention is to have single inverted commas for the direct speech and double inverted commas for the title.

American usage always reverses the single and double inverted commas, as in:

> "Hot Rocket's last hit, 'Galaxy Babe', was awesome. I can't wait for 'I Wanna Fire Your Rocket'," said Sundeep.

Note:

— remember that quotation marks are like a picture frame. Don't let anything come between them and what they are framing.
— the rest of the punctuation is straightforward.

Quiz 25

Quotes within quotes

Put single inverted commas round direct speech and double inverted commas round titles or quotations.

Tales of the Whole Nut Café

1. I love those old Frank Sinatra songs, said Miranda dreamily. My favourite is I've Got You Under My Skin.
2. My mum likes musicals, said Peaches. She made me take her to *Porgy and Bess* and she sang along to Summertime. We nearly got thrown out.
3. My Great Aunt Flora got thrown out for singing, once, said Miranda. She told them, What's the point of being old if you can't be embarrassing?
4. Sundeep chipped in, Kids can be embarrassing, too. My little brother writes songs called things like Hello to Sunshine and My Pyjama Panda. But the worst one is Sundeep's My Special Hero.
5. You poor chap! exclaimed Neil in sympathy. Do you actually let him perform Sundeep's My Special Hero?
6. Can't stop him, said Sundeep mournfully. The *Gazette* wrote an article about him called Brotherly love in Bagshaw Close.

(Answers on page 195)

4. Inverted commas used ironically

This use mirrors conversation very closely. People change tone when they are reporting something which they doubt is true. You will often see people drawing inverted commas in the air to show that they are sceptical or mocking. You can use inverted commas to give the same impression on the printed page. We could call it the 'so-called' use.

✐ EXAMPLE

It was after Grimbald divorced her that Matilda entered her 'liberated' phase.

The inverted commas round 'liberated' indicate that the writer does not think this is true liberation although clearly that is what Matilda believes and has been saying.

The Dairyman's Disaster
or Did You Really Mean That?

'Fresh' Cream from 'Contented' Cows

This was spotted in a dairy in Inverness but we have seen similar examples in supermarkets, hairdressers and market stalls round the country. It is up there with the Greengrocers' Apostrophe.

People who write notices sometimes think that putting inverted commas round certain words is like emphasizing them with twinkling lights. However, because of the 'so-called' use, it turns the word or phrase into the exact opposite, namely, *so-called fresh* and *so-called contented.* Far from intensifying the message, it casts doubt on it.

Quiz 26

'So-called' or not?

We have put in some inverted commas — are they right? If so, what do they make the sentence mean?

Tales of the Whole Nut Café

1. Arabella was determined that Neil should take her to the dance and, after three hours of her 'gentle persuasion', he was almost ready to cave in.
2. Peaches was coming round to Neil. She no longer called him Neil 'Hopeless-but-he-Tries' Findlay.
3. We will 'clean' your carpets. Satisfaction 'guaranteed'.
4. After a weekend with the Aquarian Starburst Dreamers, Miranda found 'enlightenment' and spent a morning realigning the café tables to pick up 'cosmic vibrations'.

(Answers on page 195)

Chapter Eleven

Paragraphs

In this chapter we cover:
1. What is a paragraph?
2. How to organize paragraphs
3. Paragraphs in the workplace

1. What is a paragraph?

[1] A paragraph is a series of sentences, usually connected by a theme or topic. It allows the writer to break up a long passage into manageable chunks, which makes it easier for the eye. The important thing is that each paragraph is about a single topic, which helps the reader to make sense of what is being said.

[2] You always start every new paragraph on a new line, even if it is only a short sentence.

[3] Sometimes you will indent the first word of the new paragraph. That is what we have done with this paragraph and what you will find in most books. Sometimes, as in business letters, although you still start the paragraph on a new line, you may choose to set the first word flush with the left margin.

[4] You have two options on spacing. By far the most usual is to have no additional space between paragraphs. Indenting the first word is enough to signal that this is a new paragraph. This is what you will find in all novels and most books and magazines. The less usual option is to leave a double-line space between paragraphs. You will find this in business letters, reports and on websites.

[5]   How long should a paragraph be? It depends. A paragraph can, in theory, be any length from one line to several pages. If you want some general guidance, it is probably best if a paragraph is not shorter than three sentences and not longer than ten lines or so. After that, it can become difficult to read.

[6]   You may have been told in school not to write paragraphs of a single sentence. Whilst this is a useful principle, nevertheless it is not an absolute rule. For instance, we have deliberately written a single sentence paragraph above, in [2]. Single paragraph sentences stand out. For this reason, journalists and novelists often use them to make a point that they want to stand out.

The series of paragraphs above is based on these ideas:
    [1] what is a paragraph?
    [2] always start on a new line
    [3] to indent or not to indent
    [4] spacing
    [5] how long should it be?
    [6] the possibility of single sentence paragraphs

Note:
You will notice that, as in most books, the first line of the first paragraph is not indented.

2. *How to organize paragraphs*

Good writing is well organized. It is worth taking a bit of trouble to plan what you are going to say, as we have done in the example. The important thing is to put what you want to say in a clear and logical order and make sure that the reader can follow you. This way of doing things is valid for reports, articles and essays.

Good writing is like taking your readers on a train from London to Edinburgh, so that's how we shall approach the subject.

The Train to Edinburgh:

The opening paragraph, where you tell your readers what you're going to cover, is like ensuring that they get on the right train (to Edinburgh) from the right station (London King's Cross). Readers need to feel confident that you know what you're doing, and they like to be told clearly where they're going. A good opening paragraph is a bit like the guard's: 'Good morning, ladies and gentlemen. Welcome aboard the 10.30 to Edinburgh, calling at Peterborough, York, Newcastle and arriving at Edinburgh Waverley at 15.30.' Now you know where the train's going, you know the stations on the way, and you know where and when it arrives.

The stations on the way can be compared to the paragraphs. These are your arguments which will back up the points you want to make. They will appear in logical order. This is important. Readers don't want to look out of the window and find that Peterborough has gone missing, or — heaven forbid — find that the train has swerved off track and the is now heading for Cornwall instead. It's very easy to wander off the point. If you keep your destination, Edinburgh, in mind, it will help you to keep on track.

Whenever the train approaches a new station, the guard makes an announcement: 'Ladies and gentlemen, the train is now approaching York.' You need this whenever you start a new point. You need to signal clearly where you are now (York) and what your new point is. Then your readers can relax. They know that you know what you're doing. You've brought them along safely so far, so they will be happy to listen to your argument.

All the arguments must follow on logically. You need to make sure that the York stuff goes in the York paragraph, the Newcastle stuff in the Newcastle paragraph, and so on. This, too, is easy to get wrong. It is worth reading your draft carefully to check that you haven't jumped from York to Newcastle and then back again. This would be very confusing for your travellers.

Your final paragraph can be compared to the train's arrival at Waverley Station, Edinburgh. Your readers need to know that they've arrived, and that the journey is over. From the writer's point of view, this means that you need a final paragraph which sums up your whole argument in a few sentences and draws the conclusion. Your readers can then get off the train knowing exactly where they are.

How to plan an article, using the Train to Edinburgh:
If you were writing an article for a travel magazine about a holiday in Italy, for instance, you would want an opening paragraph telling your readers what you were going to talk about: travel, where to stay, eating out, what to see, and shopping.

Already you have an opening paragraph and five topics. It would be unlikely that you could say everything you wanted to about travel, say, in one paragraph — it would be far too long, and your readers would get bored and stop reading. So you subdivide the topics into separate paragraphs to make them easier to read.

If you drew up a plan of your article, it might look like this:

1. Opening paragraph
Telling the reader what topics you will be covering.

2. Travel
 Flying
 Trains
 Car hire

3. Where to stay
 Hotels
 Self-catering

4. Eating out
 Expensive
 Moderate
 Budget

5. What to see
 Places of historical interest
 Gardens, famous views, and so on
 Don't miss: Flower Festival at end of May

6. Shopping
 Street markets

Clothes
Leatherwork
Specialities of the area

7. **Final paragraph**

This sums up everything you've said and ends with a sentence or two giving a final overview.

Example of a final paragraph:

Although San Piero is not an easy place to get to and the facilities of some of the smaller hotels are pretty basic, nevertheless this is a charming, unspoilt, typically Umbrian town. There is a reasonably priced trattoria on every corner and the local speciality *agnello arrosto* is to die for. There is lots for children to explore in the Palazzo gardens, and adults will appreciate the spectacular views from the Temple of Diana. Everybody will enjoy the Flower Festival, not to mention the violet creams and candied rose petals for sale outside the church of San Piero. This is a holiday for all the family.

So, you have seventeen paragraphs in all. Depending on how long your article is, you might want to subdivide it further. For example, for a women's magazine you might want to divide up the clothes paragraphs into two, one about knitwear and one about silks.

Topic sentences:

The important thing to remember is that each paragraph has its own topic. Often there will be a *topic sentence,* which sums up what the paragraph is about. In the *Example of a final paragraph* above, the topic sentence is: *This is a holiday for all the family.* We have put it at the end, but it could go just as well at the beginning, or possibly after the first sentence. The choice is yours.

Quiz 27

Topic sentences

Find the topic sentence in each of the following paragraphs and underline it.

Tales of the Whole Nut Café

1. The moment Neil accepted Arabella Castle's invitation to her birthday party, she rushed out and bought the sexiest dress in a slinky red satin with a plunging neck-line. She talked her father into having a marquee on the lawn and then booked the Hot Rocket Band to play. She would make sure that, before the evening was out, she had shown Neil that they were right for each other. Her plan to become Mrs Neil Findlay was looking good.

2. Peaches was competent in most ways: she was efficient, intelligent and good at dealing with the customers. Her one weak spot was mice. She had never liked them and had taken great care about the kitchen hygiene at the café. When, therefore, she saw a mouse scuttling across the floor late one evening as they were closing, she shrieked and jumped up on to a

chair, where she wobbled precariously on her high heels.

3. Neil stepped in and took control. He took one look at the mouse and saw that it was a field mouse. It must have come in from outside, he decided; he'd noticed a small hole by the back door earlier. He made a note to ring the Council Pest Control in the morning, ordered Sundeep to plug the hole with a bit of wire wool, dropped a tea towel over the frightened mouse and released it outside.

4. Peaches got down from the chair and slumped on to one of the kitchen stools. She rummaged around for the cooking sherry and poured herself a large glass. Peaches hardly ever drank and the alcohol went straight to her head. She began to hiccup. She tried to stop but it was no good. In between fright and hiccups she started to giggle. Within a couple of minutes she was hysterical and when Neil came in she was laughing, crying and hiccuping all at the same time.

5. Neil could never find the right words when talking to Peaches, or the words he did say came out all wrong. She was so quick and bright that she made him feel like a clumsy clodhopper. Whenever she came into the room he found his heart beginning to beat faster and he felt light-headed and breathless. In short, every time he saw her, Neil found himself tied up in knots.

6. This time, things were different. After releasing the mouse, Neil came into the kitchen, pulled Peaches up from the stool, put his arms round her and held her tightly. He began to tell her how beautiful she was and, gradually, he could feel her sobs quieten. Eventually Peaches was silent. Then she looked up and gave him a watery smile. Neil felt his heart turn over.

(Answers on page 196)

Quiz 28

Organizing your material

When newspapers publish an obituary of a famous person, they follow a pattern:

1. first explain what the person was most famous for
2. then what happened in the rest of their lives
3. and give a brief biographical summary to finish

Read the following obituary article. All the information is there but it is in the wrong order. Put the article right by numbering the paragraphs in the right order. It may help if you ask yourself:

— Which paragraph would make the best introduction?
— Are there any paragraphs which are so closely linked they should follow each other?
— Which is the summing up paragraph?

Dragon Deeds

The Dragon Gazette announces
the death of Athelstan Silverwing

[1]   In spite of his love of traditional ways, Silverwing was a forward-looking dragon and supported she-dragons' equal opportunities. Matilda Hurstpank said of him: "When I first began to lecture on she-dragons' rights, Athelstan taught me voice production. I owe him a lot. He will be much missed."

[2]   In return for his fire-breathing, the bats brought back honey nectar from the moonflowers on Ben Eldris. Silverwing claimed that the honey nectar contributed to his long life and health.

[3]   Athelstan Silverwing was born an only dragon to elderly parents in Bats' Cave, Ben Eldris, Caledonia. Although he went to Cumbria as a young dragon and trained as a scale-polisher, his heart was always in Ben Eldris, and after his wife died and his dragonlets had grown up, he returned there. He leaves four sons and a daughter. He was 243 years old.

[4]   Silverwings are unusual in having four nostrils, the top two are capable, with practice, of producing sound at a very high frequency and it was by this means that Athelstan Silverwing communicated with the bats. He learnt the art of bat-whistling from his grandfather. Although he encouraged his children and grandchildren to follow in his footsteps, none of them have done so.

[5]   In later years, he was well-known for running the Beltane Festival, which he did with great efficiency. Silverwing also introduced a number of exciting new

events at the Festival, such as the first years' wing-flapping competition.

[6]   The death yesterday of Athelstan Silverwing brings to an end an ancient tradition of dragon-bat co-operation. Every evening, before the bats left his cave in Ben Eldris, he would breathe out a huge plume of flame to frighten away predators hoping for an easy meal as the bats took their evening flight.

[7]   His eldest grandson, Rollo Silverwing, told our reporter: "Yeah, I can whistle with my top nostrils if I want to. It's good for keeping off the midges. But there's no way I'm living in a damp cave talking to a load of bats."

(Answers on page 197)

(Answers on page 197)

Quiz 29

Removing irrelevant information

Read the following article. Some of the information is off the point. Put brackets around what is irrelevant.

CASANOVA ON LOVE

Been thinking of my three favourite ways to seduce the ladies. Hm, difficult choice. I think they have to be: over a meal, in a gondola, and at the theatre or opera. They are all good, but each must be carefully matched with the lady. My friend Lorenzo says that I am wasting my time — but, poor fellow, he is nowhere near as successful as I am.

The meal, ah! the meal. First, the wine must be care-fully chosen. For my money, there's nothing to beat a fine champagne. The taste lingers on the palate and slips down like velvet and the bouquet alone is enough to make her think of love. Lorenzo, the greedy sot, drinks himself under the table, even when with a lady. No wonder I seduced his wife so easily. Next, some black olives to pop into her mouth. Then some poultry. Once she has nibbled at a leg and you have fed her with tasty morsels of breast, she will be squirming and giggling. Quails are good. They are small and you can suck the juice off her fingers.

Then there's the gondola. The night is dark and starry and the wind balmy. You hand her into the gondola, taking care to squeeze her fingers lightly. You sink down on to the soft cushions. The lady feels safe; she can see out — but not be seen. The gondolier sings softly — well paid, you may be sure. Stefano, the Sicilian gondolier, knows all the gossip; it was he who told me about the duke suffering from piles. Your arm goes round her and she gives a squeak, which you ignore. Such protests are for form only. You kiss and caress her, undoing the small buttons slowly. By the time you have reached your palazzo, she's soft and melting like a honey cake.

In winter, a box at the theatre or opera is as good as a gondola, and warmer, too. Nobody disturbs you and the music enhances the mood of love. A box is ideal for writing poetry, too. You need to remember to bring a small lantern, quill pen and ink, and paper. I've often found it most inspirational. For ladies, the technique is much the same as in a gondola. Move your chair close to her and, after allowing some time for the music to awaken her amatory feelings, you will soon be engaging in delicious familiarities. The music will drown out her moans and sighs. Some boxes have a divan at the back so that you may finish the business in comfort. If you time it right — not difficult for a man of my accomplishment

— then, as the music swells to climax, so can you — and your fair companion, too, naturally.

(Answers on page 199)

If you are writing a novel or a short story, you may *want* a character to wander off the point, like the talkative Miss Bates in Jane Austen's *Emma*. It is a very good indicator of character. If you are writing a mystery, it can also be a useful way of slipping in essential information discreetly.

3. Paragraphs in the workplace

Now you know how to construct and order paragraphs, let's look at how they are used at work.

The standard style for books and magazines (British and American, fiction and non-fiction) is:
— one paragraph follows another without a double-line space;
— each paragraph starts on a new line and is indented (which you can do by using the Tab key).

By contrast, the standard style for letters is:
— a double-line space between paragraphs;
— no indentation, each paragraph starts flush with the left-hand margin.

This helps the reader to see clearly where each new subject begins. Try to avoid very long paragraphs. They tire the eyes.

**Dreadnought Building and Decorating
Station Yard
Easter Findlay**

Mr Neil Findlay
Whole Nut Café
The Peebles
Easter Findlay

April 17, 20---

Dear Mr Findlay

Guttering and brickwork

This letter is to confirm our discussion of last Thursday and to submit my firm's estimate for the work required which is enclosed.

I have inspected the exterior walls and roof at the Whole Nut Café, as requested, and have to report that all the guttering at the back of the premises needs to be replaced immediately. It is badly corroded and the joints have weakened over a number of years. This has allowed water seepage into the store-room area.

The guttering at the front, however, is new and although one joint should be replaced, it is generally sound. The guttering and pipes should be cleared regularly of leaves and waste material and this had not been done. My firm would be happy to do this, too, for an additional fee. This is set out separately in the enclosed estimate.

If the estimate is acceptable to you, please indicate which works you require, sign and return one copy to me, together with a cheque for the deposit (30% of works requested), as set out in the estimate. I will then get in touch to arrange a date for the work to start.

With best wishes.

Yours sincerely

Tom Dreadnought

Points to note:

(i) It is important to plan the paragraphs in a letter, too. Here the plan is:

— Paragraph 1: the writer says why he is writing
— Paragraph 2: the bad news
— Paragraph 3: the good news
— Paragraph 4: what the recipient needs to do next if he wants the work done.

(ii) You see, too, that the letter has a subject heading, Guttering and brickwork, which tells the reader immediately what the letter is about. This is very common in business.

Quiz 30

Setting out a business letter

Put information in paragraphs and paragraphs in the proper order in a business letter.

Tales of the Whole Nut Café

Miranda is planning a letter to promote the Whole Nut Café to a local Foodies' Club. How many paragraphs do you think she should have and what should be in each? What should be the heading of the letter? Below is her basic information:

1. lemon sole with a mousseline of home-grown fennel and local elderflower wine
2. need to know dietary requirements in advance
3. £25 a head for parties of seven or fewer
4. fully organic
5. new room available for large groups
6. complimentary glass of champagne on arrival
7. bookings to miranda@thewholenutcafe.co.uk or telephone ...
8. we can do special diets, allergies etc.
9. 10% discount on parties of eight
10. gourmet menu starts Tuesday 12 June for the rest of that week

(Answers on page 200)

The business report

A business report can be written in a number of ways. Remember that time is money, so keep it as short as you can.

You can help the busy reader by putting all the main points into a single paragraph at the start of the report. This is called an Executive Summary. It should give enough information for the reader to work out how much of the whole report he needs to read in detail.

Always write a report with an end-user in mind. Who asked you to write it? What did he/she want to know and why? If you are asked to make recommendations, start off with them, perhaps as bullet points (see Chapter 5, page 74). You must set out your reasons but you can do it later in the report. This contrasts with an academic essay, where you set out your arguments first and only draw your conclusions at the end.

Again, you will find the double-line space between paragraphs helpful. It may also be sensible to number paragraphs, so you can refer the reader back to them easily.

One thing which can be difficult in writing business reports is that you may have to cover a number of topics which have no natural progression. So you could choose to order your paragraphs in any one of a number of ways. Don't worry about it. There are probably lots of options, all equally right. The important things to ensure are:

— that you have a plan;
— that it is consistent;
— that it has a place for everything you want to say;
— that you don't repeat yourself unnecessarily (to avoid this, perhaps label topics and/or number paragraphs for easy reference).

✐ EXAMPLE

You work for Scentworks, a small company which sells herbal preparations by post. Your immediate boss asks you to do a six-monthly review of the performance of the carriers which the firm uses to deliver products to customers and to recommend changes. Your boss says that she will send your report to all the Directors and to the Operational Managers.

You have done the research. Now you have a load of statistics and various bits of additional information from lots of sources, for instance, customers' complaints, conversations with the carriers themselves, and records kept by the Scentworks marketing department.

Your plan might include:

— *delivery times:* you need to say how you're measuring delivery performance, what is the best, what is the worst, what is the average by carrier
— *delivery cost:* what is the price charged by various carriers? How do they compare? Are there any better rates which could be achieved by, say, shipping only once a week in larger batches to only one carrier?
— *delivery efficiency:* do the goods arrive at the right place in the right time and in good condition?

There is no logical order in which to place these paragraphs. (Indeed, there may be so much information on each you have to break each subject heading up into several paragraphs.) You have to decide which is the most important. Keep referring back to the original brief. (Remember, you were asked to make recommendations.) Think about your different readers. Tell them where to find supporting details in your report, but don't make them read every detail, if they don't need to. By now, you know more about this than anyone — be kind to your readers.

One way of writing this report might be:

To: Ms Golightly, Manager, Customer Services

Review of Delivery of Scentworks' Products to Customer Jan–Jun, 20—

1. Executive Summary

You asked us to review the performance of our three carriers and to advise on changes for the next six months.

We continue to use three carriers, Flash PLC, Bang International and Wallop and Sons, a local firm. All are competitively priced (paragraph 4 below). Wallop and Sons are by far the most satisfactory on all counts, cost, promptness and efficiency, as long as the goods are shipped within a hundred-mile radius. In addition, they achieve high customer satisfaction. They have no capacity to take more of our business or to ship to greater distances (section 5).

The other two carriers have areas of weakness: industrial action at Flash PLC delayed our deliveries by up to two weeks in January (paragraph 3); and Bang International is seeking to impose a surcharge on their quoted price which we are currently disputing (paragraph 4). Bang is reaching an acceptable standard on delivery times and cost. There have been a number of customer complaints about the condition of parcels delivered by Flash who have, in addition, misdelivered or lost an unacceptably high level of our shipments in this half year (paragraph 5).

We recommend:
- Continuing to use Wallop & Sons as a priority
- Dividing other business between Flash PLC and Bang International
- Negotiating price robustly with Bang
- Monitoring customer satisfaction with Flash closely
- Seeking quotes from other carriers.

2. Recommendations

You have already set out your outline recommendations in your executive summary. This is the place to expand on those bullet points, for instance, put in any relevant deadlines, like expiry dates on contracts, notice periods, and so on.

You might want to continue the main body of the report using the following model:

3. Delivery Times

Details of each firm's performance, including customer comments and, perhaps, a comparison of all three in tabulated form.

4. Delivery Cost

Individual pricing schedules, changes over the half year, disputes, individual circumstances like the strike at Flash, hidden costs, comparison between the three. Rates prevailing in the industry.

5. Delivery Efficiency

Condition of parcels, proportion which go to the right address first time, flexibility in sorting out mistakes, customer response. Limitations, for instance, capacity, geographical reach.

Note:

The important thing is to realize that your report *must* be organized in a way that makes it easy to read and understand; and it must also be easy to go back to and find information readily. So give your readers a clear road map.

A final word of advice:

Remember that most institutions will have their own conventions when it comes to writing letters and reports. Our advice to you is follow them slavishly; this is no place for originality. Any letter which goes out reflects on the organization. As for internal reports, your employer will have reasons for their choice of conventions. Keeping to the same basic model makes individual reports easier to research and compare.

Big companies and institutions will have a Guide to House Style. Make sure you are aware of their rules and conventions. If there is no printed guide, ask someone reliable to show you good examples of what has been done before and copy those.

Chapter Twelve

A Brief Tour of Grammar

For most people, grammar is somewhere between science fiction and cricket. Like the best science fiction, it looks at something very familiar (words) from a completely different perspective. Like cricket, its rules are complicated and not always what you expect. Like cricket, some people can be passionate (and unreasonable) about it. Think of it as sort of Quidditch, if it helps.

You do not have to know everything about grammar in order to write well. Many of the best writers are instinctive in their choices. But you may feel a bit more confident if you know the basic terms.

NOUN: the name of a thing, person, place or idea, for instance:
— *nut, woman, café* (common nouns);
— *crowd, herd* (collective nouns i.e. names of groups);
— *patience, music, thought* (abstract nouns i.e. the names of things you can't see);
— *Miranda, Paris, Japan, London Bridge* (proper nouns, that is, names of an individual person or place). They take capital letters. See Chapter 9 (page 112) on capital letters.

PRONOUN: short words that stand instead of a noun or several nouns, for instance: *I, me, you, he, him, she, her, it, they, them, who, which.*

VERB: doing or being words which show what nouns or pronouns do. We find a useful test for identifying a verb is to see whether we can take it out of the sentence and put 'to' in front of it, for instance, *to grow, to work, to be, to become.*

ADJECTIVE: describes a noun, for instance: *hard* apple, *ambitious* woman, *new* idea, *important* law.

ADVERB: usually answers the question 'how?' and often ends in *-ly.* It says more about:
— a verb, for instance: dance *beautifully,* ride *well;*
— an adjective, for instance: *surprisingly* ambitious;
— an adverb, for instance: *very speedily.*

INTERJECTION: an exclamation; usually starts a sentence or stands alone, for instance: *Whoops! Ouch! Cor! Note:* they are usually followed by an exclamation mark (!).

PREPOSITION: linking word which say something about the relationship between things or ideas, for instance: *at, in, on, to, by, from.*

CONJUNCTION: joining word, for instance: *and, or, but, because.*

ARTICLE: definite article: *the;* indefinite article: *a, an.*

Extra Help

The following sections deal with topics which are not strictly punctuation at all. But they will help you avoid some of the elephant traps that lie in wait for writers. We hope you enjoy them.

The Learner Driver's Guide to Punctuation

Punctuation	Breathing	What it does	The L Driver's Guide
New paragraph	Long pause. Deep breath.	End of one person speaking or one set of ideas. Take stock before moving on to the next speech or set of ideas.	Halt, put on hand brake, consider route, take new direction.
Full stop	Decided pause. Fairly deep breath.	End of single idea. Small rest before starting the next single idea.	Stop. Go into neutral gear before starting again.
Colon	Decided pause.	End of first statement — there is a lot more to come.	Stop. Go immediately into first gear to do the next bit.
Semi-colon	Slow down and pause, with a quick breath in order to take you on immediately after each semi-colon.	You are setting out complicated ideas, in small parcels, there is more to come after each semi-colon.	You are on a straight road with several sets of traffic lights. Pace yourself and you won't have to jump red lights or stop. But you will have to slow down to a crawl as you approach red or amber lights, while still preparing to go through as soon as they turn green.

Brackets	Distinct break but no pause, change tone, maybe speed up.	You are inserting a supplementary idea.	You may notice something but don't take your eyes off the road!
Dashes	Distinct break, maybe change expression.	You are commenting, maybe even contradicting.	Swear at the other driver if you want but *don't* take your eyes off the road!
Single dash	EITHER small pause, to emphasize the next point OR abrupt stop.	Something additional occurs to you or you come to an abrupt halt.	EITHER you go down into second gear as you check the signpost OR you jam on the brakes.
Comma	Smallest pause, quick breath.	You are putting the text into manageable chunks.	You've slowed down but you know where you're going and are ready to accelerate.
Hyphen	No pause at all.	The hyphen tells you to run two words together.	There's no one on the pedestrian crossing, go right ahead!

Word Traps and Confusions

Dear J & E

I want to go into advertising but I've been to a careers person and he says I'm no good because of my vocabulary. What does he mean? Is he right? What can I do about it?
Jo

Dear Jo

Your vocabulary is the stock of words you use. (The Anglo-Saxons called it 'word hoard' which sums it up well.)

Nobody uses all the words in the English language. The ones you choose say a lot about you.

The best thing to do to improve your vocabulary is to read widely. Maybe you could adopt a word for a day, if it is new to you? Take it out for exercise — and get some friends to join in!

Have fun!
J & E

Choosing the right words

Choosing the right words is a very great skill. We go on learning it all our lives. If you want to write well, always consider your reader. Which words will help him or her understand your point?

George Orwell, in his *Politics and the English Language,* said you should never use a long word where a short one will do. We agree. Long words can be a way of showing off.

They can also be a smokescreen. If you don't really know what you are talking about, it is easier to hide it with long, vague words than short, precise ones. Before you can choose the right words, you must know your subject.

George Orwell also said you should never use a foreign phrase, scientific word or jargon where you can think of an everyday English equivalent.

JARGON: of course, some professions have their own specialized vocabulary. If you are a doctor writing to another doctor, you are entitled to use a precise term which you both recognize. If, however, you are writing for the general public, specialist terms and jargon carry an unfriendly message: I am cleverer than you; you are not a member of this exclusive club.

Wrong words and how to avoid them

All through this book we have been saying, 'Be kind to your reader'. This is where we say, 'Be kind to yourself, too.' People judge you by what you write. Some of them care an awful lot about wrong use of words. Don't give them ammunition.

Elephant trap: 'I and me'

You hear this mistake all the time. It even gets into print. (If you want to know why it is a mistake, have a look at a book on grammar.) People who care about such things will notice.

'Cherie and I are delighted to be here.' ✔

'The Press Liaison Officer told Cherie and I to sit on the platform.' ✘

'Thank you for thinking of Cherie and I.' ✘

'You have all been so welcoming to Cherie and I.' ✘

The rule of thumb is to take out the other person's name and see whether it still sounds right. Apart from the first example, they all need 'me'. We don't think anyone would say,

'The Press Liaison Office told I to sit on the platform.' ✘

'Thank you for thinking of I.' ✘

'You have all been so welcoming to I.' ✘

Okay, yes, you creative writers, we know about Lorelei Lee. The whole point of her phrase 'A girl like I' was that, though uneducated, she was shrewd and gorgeous and got her man — who obviously thought other things were more important.

Terrible twos: word confusion

There are many pairs of words which are often muddled. You will hear the wrong word used often. You can probably add others of your own. Our advice? If in doubt, look it up. A dictionary is a wonderful security blanket. Some of the commonest are:

AFFECT and EFFECT: *affected* means 'influenced by', *effected* means 'achieved' or 'done'. An *effect* is an 'outward manifestation' (like the Doppler effect).

BLOND and BLONDE: this is from the French. *Blonde* is simply the feminine form of *blond.* In practice, the feminine form is used most of the time in English, unless you are referring to a fair-haired man e.g. Mark was a blond.

BOUGHT and BROUGHT: *bought* comes from 'to buy' e.g., I bought a pretty pair of earrings. *Brought* comes from 'to bring' e.g. I brought my new earrings downstairs to show my friend.

COMPLEMENT and COMPLIMENT: *complement* means 'complete', as in 'the full complement of cutlery'; *to complement* means 'to make whole'; *complementary* means something which completes the set or the whole. *Compliment,* on the other hand, means praise.

DIFFUSE and DEFUSE: apparently the commonest word muddle in the UK. *Diffuse* most commonly means 'widespread', even 'too widespread' and so 'confused, vague'. *Defuse* means 'to remove the fuse' and therefore 'to make harmless'.

DISCREET and DISCRETE: *discreet* means 'wisely cautious', particularly about saying things. A discreet person can be trusted to keep a secret. *Discrete* means 'detached or distinct', as in 'a discrete line of questioning in this case'.

DISINTERESTED and UNINTERESTED: *disinterested* means you have no advantage to gain in the outcome. An umpire or an adjudicator should be disinterested. *Uninterested* means bored.

FLAUNT and FLOUT: *flaunt* means to display something about oneself ostentatiously — you might flaunt a new engagement ring, for example. *Flout* means to express contempt and, in particular, to ignore a rule or law.

IMPLY and INFER: these two are a mirror image. IMPLY is to mean something additional which you don't say. INFER is to interpret an additional meaning which has not been said. Gurus imply. Paranoiacs infer.

LOOSE and LOSE: this is simply a spelling error. *Loose* means unbound, free, as in 'loose hair'; maybe too free, as in 'loose woman'. *Lose* means that you can't find something as in 'I lose track', 'to lose a game'.

PASSED and PAST: *passed* is a doing word, for example 'he passed an exam' or 'You passed the signpost'. *Past* means gone by or over, as in 'past, present and future' or 'The bus went past too quickly for me to see the number'.

PRACTICE and PRACTISE: in British English, practice is the correct spelling for the noun in all its senses: *to do football practice, a medical practice.* The spelling for the verb to practise is slightly different, as we see: *to practise medicine, to practise in the gym.* In American usage, however, the same spelling, practice, is used for both noun and verb.

PRINCIPAL and PRINCIPLE: *principal* means first in rank or money. It could be the Head of a school, for example, or the amount of a loan before all the interest is added. *Principle* means a fundamental truth or law, for example 'a point of principle'.

STATIONARY and STATIONERY: *stationary* means standing still. *Stationery* means writing materials. We have found we can remember which is which by saying that stationery is sold by a stationer — and then just add 'y' to the shopkeeper.

THERE, THEIR and THEY'RE: *there* is a place. It may help you if you think of 'here and there'. *Their* means 'belonging to them'. *They're* means 'they are'.

WHO'S and WHOSE: this is similar to 'it's' and 'its'. *Who's* means 'who is'. *Whose* means 'who that belongs to', e.g. 'Whose breeches are those?' demanded Donna Caterina's father.

Weasel words

YOUTH SLANG: it can be equally divisive when generations colonize words. A new stepmother we know was horrified to hear her husband's son tell his friends that she was 'wicked'. In teenager terms, of course, it was a great compliment.

New slang appears all the time. A recent invention is 'bling bling' meaning 'expensive, ostentatious stuff', or 'minger' which is 'an unattractive woman'.

Some phrases, of course, are just meaningless, even with a local guide. 'I'm — like — wow — that's so — know what I'm saying?' still has us puzzled.

> ### 🔴 Careful! ✎
>
> If you use new slang in a novel, make sure that your reader knows what you mean from the context. Words like this may not last long!

Spin

Politicians and advertisers use words to say one thing and mean another. As a result, people have become cynical about trusting these professions. For example, 'Let me be absolutely clear,' is usually a good signal that here comes a careful cloak for every point on which the speaker feels vulnerable. If you're a politician, you may find them useful. Otherwise, be careful.

Coded words

People often take refuge behind coded language rather than give offence. For example, 'Return a robust answer' is code for 'Tell them to go away' — or worse. One of the most delightful of these is 'Up to a point, Lord Copper'. That was the only way in which staff were allowed to disagree with Lord Copper, the newspaper magnate, in Evelyn Waugh's novel, *Scoop*.

Shape shifters

Language is fluid. Take the word *presently*. Originally it meant what it ought to mean: 'at once'. (In North America it still does.) However, four centuries of teenage boys saying they 'will take the rubbish out presently' has changed this to: 'in an unspecified number of minutes or hours, always provided that I don't forget'.

Three of the commonest shape shifters are:

ALL RIGHT (preferable) and ALRIGHT (acceptable spelling according to Oxford English Dictionary): we confess — we hate 'alright' and never use it. Yet there is a television programme called 'Alright on the Night' which doesn't seem to worry other people.

FARTHER and FURTHER: both mean 'going beyond'. For years *farther* was used to mean distance, as in 'far, farther, farthest'. *Further* was used when describing ideas or time — as in 'further confusion', 'further delay'. These days this distinction seems to be falling away.

DECIMATE: we all have our pet peeves, and this is one of ours. The root of the word is the same as 'decimal' and it literally means to reduce by a tenth. If a Roman legion mutinied, the punishment was to *decimate* them, or 'to select by lots and put to death one in ten'. Now that might be a lot of people, but ninety per cent were left standing. It wasn't extermination. These days, however, *decimate* is widely used to mean something close to 'wipe out'.

171

Some people resist all change and some people take a special dislike to one particular change. Do not let other people's pet peeves worry you. You can't please everyone. Consult a dictionary and if it says you're using the word properly, stop worrying.

A final word of advice:

If someone uses a word that you do not understand, be brave and ask. Reasonable people are always happy to explain. If they are not, you will often find they do not understand the word themselves. Many terms come into fashion by being copied by people who do not bother to find out what they mean.

A Guide to Presenting Manuscripts

Publishers receive hundreds of manuscripts a week. Their offices are piled high with the things. They are looking for ways to weed out the no-hopers. One way to get your book weeded out before it's even been read is to present it in an amateur way.

Rumour says, and it is probably true, that, on average, any typescript sent in to a publisher or agent gets, at the most, two minutes' notice. It is vital that you make a good impression right from the first page.

Presentation

1. The book needs to be typed on a decent word processing package.
2. It has to be easy to read, so use a clear typeface, nothing fancy, curly or Gothic. We suggest Times New Roman or similar. Don't give the reader eye-strain: use a good-sized font — 12 point is best.
3. The typescript must be on one side of the paper only and with *double-line spacing*. This is because double-line spacing is easier to read.
4. *Don't* leave additional line spaces between paragraphs, unless you want to show a change of scene mid-chapter. In other words, your text should be continuous.
5. Allow a wide margin — about $1\frac{1}{4}$ to $1\frac{1}{2}$ inches (3 to 4 cm) all round. The reader may want to write 'brilliant!' in the margin.
6. When you type, the text automatically lines up neatly on the left. This is called 'justifying left'. Do *not* justify

the text on the right-hand side— that is, leave that edge higgledy-piggledy.

7. Indent each new paragraph by about half an inch (1 cm), except for the first paragraph of a chapter or section, which you should line up with the left-hand margin.

8. Number pages consecutively. That is, don't go back to page 1 for Chapter 2, even though you may choose to set up a new file document for Chapter 2. Your word processing package will let you start a new document on a page number of your choice. For example, in Word, you click on Insert; then on Page Numbers; then on Format and enter the page number you want in 'start at'.

9. There may be an accident and the reader drops your book; pages scatter everywhere. The reader has to be able to put it back together again easily. So you should have a running header on every page which gives the name of the book and the author. Your word processing package will enable you to do this: in Word, you click on View and then on Header and Footer and enter the title of your choice as a header.

10. Begin each chapter on a new page.

11. Put the title and your name (or pseudonym) on the Title Page. You should also give your name, postal and email address and telephone number, and the approximate number of words. It's a good idea to include the date of submission, so the publisher or agent has a twinge of conscience if she/he has kept it too long. (*Note:* always print off a new title page for a new submission and, of course, alter the date. If you think your typescript is looking shabby, print off a fresh one.)

12. By the time you have got this far, your punctuation should be fine! Grammar and spelling are important too, so revise carefully for errors. They do matter.

Packing and Sending

1. *Do not* staple or pin pages together or separate chapters into plastic folders. It just means more fuss for the reader.
2. *Do not* use ring binders or other fastenings. When an agent or publisher is reading a typescript she/he might want to take a wodge of it away to read and to have it in a ring binder is not helpful.
3. Keep the pages together with a strong elastic band. If you want to put it in something, use a wallet folder, clearly labelled with your name and the title of the book.
4. Post the manuscript in a strong padded envelope. *Do not* put your typescript in a box, such as an old typing paper box. Boxes have sharp edges and can rip even the most solid padded envelopes.

Courtesy

1. Include either stamps or a cheque to cover return postage and a self-addressed label.
2. *Do not* record delivery or register the packet. It makes more work for the agent or publisher. Keep a Proof of Posting slip for yourself (free from the Post Office) and enclose a stamped self-addressed postcard for the publisher/agent to acknowledge receipt of the typescript.
3. It can easily take an agent or editor 3–4 months to get round to reading your typescript, so don't hold your breath. Get on with the next book!

Estimating the number of words

Your word processing package will give you a word count. In MS Word, for example, you click on Tools and then Word Count. This is fine for most publishers, certainly when you submit your first work, when all they need is a rough idea of how many printed pages your typescript would turn into.

In preparing a typescript for publication, publishers use a system of averages which also takes account of the white space between the words. Computer word counts give the exact number of words, but do not allow for the white space.

This is how you calculate the white space word count:
  1. Count the number of words in 20 lines that stretch across the whole page (i.e. not the final line of a paragraph or short lines of dialogue) e.g. 220 words in 20 lines.
  2. Divide by twenty for the average number of words per line, e.g. 12 words per line.
  3. Multiply by the total number of lines in a full page, e.g. $12 \times 32 = 384$
  4. Multiply this figure by the total number of pages, e.g. $384 \times 200 = 76\ 800$ words

Computer word count is always shorter than white space word count. It is important to remember this, if you are targeting a publisher's series which has a rigid word limit.

Answers to Quizzes

Quiz 1

Is this a sentence? (see page 12)

1. Don't trust a smooth-talking man. ✔
2. Donna Teresa received a love letter. ✔
3. If she stepped out on to her balcony at midnight ✗

* Not a sentence because it does not make sense on its own. Examples of true sentences which make sense might be:

— If she stepped out on to her balcony at midnight, Casanova would be waiting with a ladder.
— If she stepped out on to her balcony at midnight, her feet would get cold.
— If she stepped out on to her balcony at midnight, she could see the stars.

4. A full moon, as big and bright as a silver plate, shone in at the bedroom window, where Donna Teresa was brushing her hair. ✔
5. Love, the great deceiver ✗

* Not a sentence because it is just a label. Complete sentences might be:

— Love is the great deceiver.
— Love, the great deceiver, can make fools of us all.
— Love, the great deceiver, is a waste of time, thought Don Marco.

6. When she heard her father's footsteps, Donna Teresa decided that she ✗

* Not a sentence because we don't know what Donna Teresa decided, so it doesn't make sense as it stands. Complete sentences might be:

— When she heard her father's footsteps, Donna Teresa decided that she dared no longer wait for Casanova.
— When she heard her father's footsteps, Donna Teresa decided that she had better hide the love letter.
— When she heard her father's footsteps, Donna Teresa decided that she would hit him over the head with a candlestick if he came in.

7. Casanova, the famous Italian lover, only seduced ladies who ✗

* Not a sentence because the statement about the ladies isn't complete. Ladies who what? Examples of a complete sentence might be:

— Casanova, the famous Italian lover, only seduced ladies who were either married or widowed.
— Casanova, the famous Italian lover, only seduced ladies who were pretty.
— Casanova, the famous Italian lover, only seduced ladies who enjoyed intelligent conversation as well as love-making.

   8. Don Marco, who had challenged Casanova to a duel ✗

* Not a sentence because we're expecting to be told more about Don Marco. Examples of a complete sentence might be:

— Don Marco, who had challenged Casanova to a duel, was an expert swordsman.
— Don Marco, who had challenged Casanova to a duel, wrote his Will.
— Don Marco, who had challenged Casanova to a duel, left for the country the next morning.

   9. Always have an alibi ready. ✔
 10. If you want to seduce someone's wife, always have an alibi ready.

                                    ✔

Quiz 2

Making a sentence (see page 15)

1. Dragons come in many colours. The fiercest are red.
2. The dragons at the meeting were specially chosen for their wisdom. It took many months to call them all together.
3. The baby dragon was laughing so much that he got hiccups. He set the bush on fire. His father told him sternly not to be so silly.
4. Dragons spend all winter burnishing their scales. When the ice melts they admire themselves in the mountain lakes.
5. The dragons were furious when the eagles came into their valley. Some of the high council wanted to go to war at once. They decided to send Ranulf Forktail to negotiate.
6. Norbert easily beat his rival Grimbald in the tail-lashing competition. Grimbald was suffering from a strained muscle that year and his tail-lashing was well below his usual standard.
7. Snow dragons live among the icy peaks. Sea dragons live in caves along the shore.
8. For many years Matilda won the annual prize for egg-laying. This year she got fed up and went off to write an article called *Egg-Laying is a Feminist Issue.*

9. When Ranulf had greeted the eagles' herald in the meadow, he went to the eagle camp to meet the leaders. They offered him their word beer to help him understand their language.
10. Ranulf believed that if you spoke loudly and clearly then everyone would understand Dragonish. He refused the word beer.

Quiz 3

Breaking up a piece of writing into sentences (see page 16)
Neil 'Hopeless-but-he-tries' Findlay

Neil spent several weeks looking for a suitable location for the Whole Nut Café. He found a beautiful shop opposite the lake in the park. He was about to sign the lease, when Peaches pointed out that it was a long way from the shopping centre and had very little parking. Her Jamaican granny always said, 'Men be stupid sometime'. So Peaches gave him a checklist and he started again. He trawled round the centre looking for a place with parking, accessible to the shops and where there was room to expand upstairs if the Whole Nut Café were successful. It had to have room inside to seat at least thirty people plus the counter and they would need room for a decent-sized kitchen at the back with parking for deliveries. He thought that Peaches was being too picky but he was no good with bossy women. He did as he was told.

Sundeep

Sundeep walked into the building site that was going to become the Whole Nut Café and asked for a job. Peaches was up a ladder so she told Neil to interview him. Flustered, Neil asked if he had had any previous experience.

Sundeep took his hands out of his pockets and said he could do anything. Cooking ran in his family. His Aunty Meera cooked the best samosas north of the border.

Neil thought that adding up might be important. He asked Sundeep how much change he would need if a customer bought two cups of coffee for 90p each, a slice of cake for £1.10 and a macaroon for 75p and offered a five pound note. He rummaged in his briefcase to find a calculator.

179

Sundeep told him not to bother. The answer was £1.35.

Neil was not sure this was the right answer but Peaches cheered loudly from the top of her ladder. He offered Sundeep the job.

Ditzy Miranda

Miranda was excited. She just knew that an organic café would be brilliant. She would wear an unbleached linen smock and perhaps fresh flowers in her hair. They would have simple meadow flowers on the tables. They could cook with plants, too. There was nasturtium salad, dandelion soufflé and rose petal sorbet. She poured out her ideas down the telephone to Peaches. She was disappointed that her friend did not seem quite as enthusiastic as she was. Still, she went to bed that night feeling very satisfied.

Sensible Peaches

Peaches left her job at the wine bar on Friday. Everyone had clubbed together to buy her a potted palm for the café. They all promised to come and taste her food as soon as the café was up and running.

The next morning she was comparing her mother's recipe for Jamaica rum cake, using dark rum, with her grandmother's, which used white rum and a lot of muscovado sugar, when the phone rang. Miranda hardly let Peaches get a word out before starting to burble about putting flowers in soups and soufflés.

She was full of ideas about decorating the food with peonies and petunias, lilac and laburnum. She said the food would look gorgeous. Everyone would be talking about the café.

Peaches said that they certainly would. Laburnum flowers were poisonous. Miranda was irritated by her lack of vision. Peaches raised her eyes to the ceiling and decided on dark rum.

Quiz 4

Commas in lists of things or qualities (see page 23)

1. Matilda decided that laying a large clutch of eggs was boring,

uncomfortable, troublesome and a waste of time for a dragon of her intelligence.

2. Speckled dragons are considered to be honest, hard-working, reliable, tireless and a bit thick.

3. Baby dragons eat heather, thistles, grubs, worms and wasps.

4. A dragon's nest is made of carefully-placed branches, pine cones, sheep's wool, pumice and several wolf skins.

5. Albreda's famous word beer needs spring water, bats' toe-nails, four rock salamanders, a pinch of fly-agaric toadstool and stirring by the light of a full moon for two days, sixteen hours, forty-two minutes and eight seconds.

6. Sea dragons are blue, green, iridescent and snake-like.

7. Norbert liked to admire his tail, scales, teeth, horns and reflection in the mountain pools.

8. Breathing out fire requires strong muscles, large lungs, breath control, practice and a good breakfast of hot coals.

9. Underneath his stodgy, pompous and bossy exterior, Ranulf Forktail was passionate, sensitive and rather shy.

10. The dragon chief's funeral was attended by Siberian snow-dragons, Atlantic sea-dragons, winged horses, two unicorns and a phoenix.

Quiz 5

Commas in lists of actions (see page 25)

1. Peaches photocopied the title deeds, took them to her solicitor, signed the lease and went to tell the others.

2. Peaches announced that she would cook, Miranda would lay the tables, Sundeep would wash up and Neil would deliver his organic vegetables by ten in the morning.

3. Neil's mother came to poke about, take stock, assess the mess Neil had got himself into this time and offer plentiful advice.

4. Miranda woke up, remembered that she had to open the café, went back to sleep, woke up again and picked up the telephone to call Peaches.

5. Peaches swept the floor several times, cleaned the big window, rearranged the tables twice and knocked over the big plate of home-made rum cake.

181

6. Sundeep liked to put on his old jeans, borrow his brother's motor-bike and ride round the town.

7. Sundeep turned on the old computer, waited a few moments, pressed the Enter key, waited even longer and sighed heavily.

8. Neil drove into town, stopped at the traffic lights, remembered that he had left the tomatoes on the doorstep, went three times round the roundabout looking for a gap in the traffic and drove back home again to pick them up.

9. Sundeep told Peaches that he had peeled all the potatoes, put out the rubbish sacks for the bin men, helped Neil bring in the day's delivery of salad, printed the week's menus, washed the floor and now he wanted a coffee.

10. Miranda searched through the newspaper, found the email address of the tourist officer, sent him a message, prowled round the office waiting for his reply, pounced on the telephone number at the bottom of his note, called him at once and arranged a meeting for the next day.

Quiz 6

Commas marking additional information (see page 27)

1. Ermintrude, the oldest dragon, kept her voice in trim by yodelling every morning.

2. Albreda, famous for her word beer, prided herself on her head for drink.

3. Norbert, the winner of the tail-lashing competition, was too vain to be a popular dragon.

4. I, Matilda, do hereby declare that I am standing for election to the Dragon Council.

5. Ranulf Forktail, the dragons' negotiator, went to see Og, king of the eagles.

6. Beltane, the dragons' spring festival, was celebrated with a huge bonfire, which was the result of many weeks' preparation.

7. The visiting dragon, who was a beautiful emerald green, said that he was named Tamerlane, after a famous king, and that he came from Sogdiana, a country thousands of miles away.

8.* The council meeting consisted of Grimbald, the fire breathing expert, Matilda, the anti-egg campaigner, and Ranulf, the chief negotiator.

* Here you still put a comma after 'campaigner', even though it is followed by 'and'. This is because you need a comma on either side of the phrase 'anti-egg campaigner,' which describes Matilda.

If we take out the additional information in this sentence, then we are back to a simple list, as set out in Section 1, and we do not need a comma before the final 'and'.

This would be written: *The council meeting comprised Grimbald, Matilda and Ranulf.*

Most lists are perfectly clear in context. For example, we believe that our readers know there were three dragons at that meeting. But it is just possible to think there were five dragons there. If you think this is a risk, be radical — rephrase or repunctuate, for example with brackets, to give you:

The council meeting consisted of Grimbald (the fire breathing expert), Matilda (the anti-egg campaigner) and Ranulf (the chief negotiator). (See Chapter 5, page 61, on Brackets)

Quiz 7

Commas for emphasis (see page 32)

1. Neil was, in fact, hopeless at adding up the till receipts correctly.
2. Miranda had been warned about cooking too much. Nevertheless, she was so excited about her four-cheese scones with added sage that she made far more than she'd intended.
3. Sensible Peaches, of course, made Neil sit down and draw up a proper business plan.
4. Neil, naturally, felt that men knew best, so he ignored Peaches's advice on the grounds that the Bank Manager was a friend of his father.
5. The Bank Manager, however, told Neil that he couldn't sanction a bank loan without a proper business plan.
6. Miranda, as you know, is a bit of an air head but she has a good heart.
7. We shall have to see, therefore, if the Whole Nut Café can open on time.
8. Sundeep knew that Peaches was reluctant to experiment with his Aunty Meera's recipe for samosas. All the same, he kept trying to persuade her.

Quiz 8

Commas when addressing someone (see page 38)

1. 'Donna Lucia, you are looking ravishing tonight.'
2. 'That is because I have just become engaged to be married, Signor Casanova.'
3. 'You're too late, my friend,' said Don Vittorio, coming up. 'The lady is betrothed to me!'
4. 'You mean, Don Vittorio, that from now on I may only admire her from afar?'
5. 'I know your reputation, Casanova. I forbid you to approach my future wife.'
6. Casanova thought, we'll see about that, my friend.
7. Donna Lucia thought, Vittorio, you are rich, noble and have just given me a vastly expensive diamond ring, but Casanova is far more attractive than you, poor toad.
6. Don Vittorio thought, I'm not sure, Lucia, that I entirely trust you.
7. Oh Love, how much stronger you are than Honour!

Quiz 9

Left-out letters (see page 44)

1. 'I'm the oldest dragon here,' said Ermintrude. 'I shouldn't have to wait.'
2. If you're entering the dragon tail-lashing competition, you'll need to practise regularly.
3. It's unusual for dragons to fall ill. Normally they're very healthy.
* *It's* — only used when it means *it is*.
4. 'Come along, there's just time for claw-clipping before supper,' said Albreda to her grandson. 'Won't,' he replied rudely.
5. He'd always hated having his claws clipped. He'd rather miss supper than have them done.
* *He'd* can mean *he had* or *he would*.
6. 'We've not had a good year,' said Ranulf Forktail. 'Only six eggs were laid, though, fortunately, they've all hatched.'
7. 'I've got better things to do than sit on eggs,' snapped Matilda. 'You'll not [*you won't* is okay, too] catch me doing it again.'

* *will not* is usually shortened to *won't*. You can, if you prefer, shorten *you will not* to *you'll not* instead of you *won't*. *You'll not* is old-fashioned. So if you are a creative writer, this form may be useful for an older character.

   8. Ranulf couldn't think of a suitably crushing reply, so he muttered, 'You've got a nerve,' in a weak way, and snorted.

Quiz 10

Ownership (see page 49)

Note: We have shown some wrong answers and explained why.

   1. Sundeep's idea of cleaning was to sweep any rubbish under the counter.
   2. The Whole Nut Café's walls were painted primrose yellow. ✔

* Wrong answer: The Whole Nut Café's *walls'* were painted primrose yellow. ✘

   This is wrong because here *walls* is an ordinary plural. The walls do not own anything. An example where an apostrophe follows *walls* might be:

   Throughout the house, the *walls' plaster* was falling off. ✔

   3. If Miranda's mother was a fuss-pot, Neil's was far worse.
   4. Miranda's recipe for ice-cream was superior to Peaches's.
   5. The women's cloakroom had fluffy pink towels. ✔

* Wrong answer: The *womens'* cloakroom had fluffy pink towels. ✘

   This is wrong because *women* is already plural. The correct form of ownership with *women* is always *women's*.

   6. Miranda and Peaches's specialities included avocado with honey and mustard dressing. ✔

* Wrong answer: Miranda and Peaches's *specialitie's* included avocado with honey and mustard dressing. ✘

   There are two things wrong with this. First, *specialitie* is not a word; the singular of *specialities* is *speciality*. Second, as with No 2 above, here *specialities* is an ordinary plural. They don't own anything. An example where *specialities* might be followed by an apostrophe is:

   In the ice cream cabinet, the specialities' section was marked with a picture of a hazel nut. ✔

7. The customers' coats were hung on a pair of antlers which Sundeep had found in a skip. ✔

* Wrong answer: The customer's coats were hung on a pair of antler's which Sundeep had found in a skip. ✗

Again, there are two things wrong here. First, *customer's coats* means that there is one customer with lots of coats. If there are lots of coats, it is more likely that there are lots of customers. Second, as with No 2 above, *antlers* is a simple plural. They are not owning anything here. An example where *antlers* might be followed by an apostrophe is:

Some of the antlers' branches were broken. ✔

8. Peaches's secret dream was to bath in asses' milk. ✔

* Wrong answer: Peaches's secret dream was to bath in *asse's* milk. ✗

This is wrong for the same reason as No 6, because *asse* is not a word. The plural is *asses* and the apostrophe goes after the last 's' in the usual way. (It does take lots of asses to deliver a bath of milk.) If we were talking about a single animal, it would be:

The ass's bridle was finely-worked local leather. ✔

9. Neil missed the meeting because he was at the Men's Singles Final at Wimbledon.

10. Sundeep was a great success as a clown at the children's party and Miranda's hedgehog-shaped cake was eaten to the last crumb.

Quiz 11

It's or its? (see page 52)

1. If a lady is early for an assignation, it's a bad sign.
2. It's a pleasing courtesy to send flowers to a lady the morning after.
3. The morning can bring its regrets.
4. If a lady sends a note, its contents may be deceptive.
5. In taking a romantic stroll, it's always advisable to ensure that the lady's pet dog is on its lead.

Quiz 12

Colons (see page 55)

1. There are many different sorts of dragons: Siberian snow dragons, Atlantic sea dragons, domestic speckled dragons and rare Caledonian blue dragons.
2. The Dragon Council Agenda was as follows: apologies for absence, agreeing the minutes of the last meeting, report on the decline in egg-laying, security for the Beltane Festival, and any other business.
3. Matilda gave a list of her forthcoming articles: 'Egg-laying is a Feminist Issue'; 'She-Dragons' Manifesto'; 'Ermintrude: A Life of Contrasts'; and 'Tail-lashing for Females'.
* Did you pick up the colon after 'Ermintrude'?
4. Memo:

To:	Og, King of the Eagles
From:	Ranulf Forktail
Re:	River boundary treaty

5. The causes of Grimbald's accident whilst fire-breathing were the following: over-eating hot coals that morning, a strong westerly wind and poor maintenance of the fire extinguishers.
6. As Albreda's little rhyme had it:

   A glass of word beer
   Will make meaning clear.
   Too much of the brew
   And the meaning's askew.

7. Tamerlane's address: 42, Temple Way, Samarkand, Sogdiana.
8. Ermintrude's catchphrase was: I can remember the time when speckled dragons knew their place.
9. For tickets for the tail-lashing competition contact: Athelstan Silverwing, Ermintrude Glop or the Administrator, Retirement home for Gentle-dragons.
10. Events at the Beltane Festival will include: fire-jumping, rock-hurling, a special performance of the Caledonian Dragons' Moon Dance and the first-years' wing-flapping competition.

Quiz 13

Semi-colons (see page 58)

1. Neil's mother said it was a pity that Peaches dressed like a tart and couldn't speak the Queen's English; Arabella Castle dressed like a lady and sounded just like the Duchess of Bywater.
2. Peaches realized that Neil could be quite cool if he cut his hair; if he got rid of that terrible old tweed jacket with the leather patches on the elbows; if he smiled at her sometimes at management meetings instead of glowering at his papers all the time; if he lightened up, for heaven's sake.
3. Miranda lost patience and told Neil some home truths: he fancied Peaches; he was too stupid to notice it but he had fancied her ever since she stood up to him at that first meeting; his mother was always dropping in to the café to check that he had not asked Peaches out on a date; hadn't he noticed any of that?
4. ❤ For the first time Neil really looked at Peaches and found he liked what he saw: the startling flash of her big brown eyes; the sensuous swish of her red mini skirt; the unexpected clatter of beads in her hair; above all, he liked the sound of her bubbling laughter.

* ❤ Semi-colons are often a matter of personal taste. It would be possible to use commas here, as the phrases are not too complicated. It's up to you.

5. Sundeep and Miranda agreed that Neil would be lucky to escape from Arabella Castle: she asked him to parties; she made her friends ask him to parties; she dropped in when he went to see his mother; and if all that failed, she pulled on her gumboots and stalked him through his own farmyard.
6. ❤ They all said that the café staff did not have time to help out at the charity picnic but Arabella refused to accept excuses: not Peaches's work schedule; not Miranda's hot date; not even Sundeep's IT skills course.

* ❤ Again, the phrases are not very complicated. Semi-colons make a longer pause than commas but you could use either.

7. It was on the picnic that Neil realized what was going on: finding Arabella sitting beside him every time he dropped to the grass for a moment; his mother beaming; Peaches not meeting his eyes as

she played noisy games with the children, her beaded hair flying, and those unsuitable clothes delectably revealing; Arabella swotting a child out of the way as she strode across the cake crumbs to get to him; Miranda looking wise; and everyone, it seemed, watching him all the time.

8. Neil saw the truth at last: Peaches was frighteningly sexy; Arabella was just frightening.

Quiz 14

Saying more than one sentence at a time (see page 79)

1. 'The reporter's called Isobel Cameron. That's obviously not her. Look at him, what a scruff!'
2. 'Come on, Neil! He's a biker, that's all.'
3. 'You're too tolerant, Peaches. He can't come in here if he's wearing a helmet.'
4. 'Honestly, you sound just like your mother sometimes. Anyway, he's taking off his helmet.'
5. 'Miranda's gone all pink! Are you OK?'
6. 'He's coming in! Where's my comb? My hair's a mess!'

Quiz 15

Punctuating conversation (see page 80)

1. Ranulf Forktail said, 'I am sorry to report that the negotiations with the eagles have broken down.'
2. 'The eagles always were troublesome,' sighed Ermintrude.
3. 'We can fight them,' put in Albreda's young nephew eagerly.
4. Albreda looked at him and replied sternly, 'There'll be no fighting, young dragon.'
5. 'The she-eagles don't want a war,' agreed Matilda.
6. Grimbald nodded and added, 'It's their egg-laying season. They'll be fearful for their eggs.'
7. 'What about sending Matilda to talk to them?' suggested Albreda.
8. 'What good would that do? She'd only lecture them on she-eagles' rights,' snorted Ranulf, flicking his wings irritably.
9. Ermintrude looked at him for a long moment and then said quietly, 'Just because you don't get on with her doesn't mean that she's not

a good negotiator. What's more she knows the she-eagles. I second Albreda's suggestion.'

10. Athelstan Silverwing rose, swished his tail a few times, and pronounced, 'Ermintrude's right. The she-eagles may be willing to talk to Matilda. It's worth a try.'

Quiz 16

Showing who is speaking when breaking up speech (see page 82)

1. 'I'm really worried that Sundeep has had an accident,' said Peaches. 'Even he isn't usually two hours late.'
2. 'What you mean,' retorted Miranda, 'is that he's never been this late before.'
3. 'Don't think you need to worry,' Neil agreed. 'He's probably overslept.'
4. 'Hi,' said Sundeep, astonished to see them all standing around the café at this time in the morning. 'Did I miss something?'
5. 'I suppose,' drawled Miranda, looking at the clock, 'it's nice to know you're not dead.'
6. 'Dead?' Sundeep echoed, puzzled. 'Why should I be dead?'
7. 'When you didn't call,' pointed out Neil, trying not to laugh, 'Peaches thought you'd fallen under a lorry.'
8. 'The least you could do,' said Miranda, 'is make up a decent excuse.'
9. 'From now on,' Peaches told Sundeep, 'you're here at nine o'clock on the dot or you get your cards.'
10. 'But Peaches,' whined Sundeep, 'that's so unfair.'

Quiz 17

Setting out speech (see page 86)

'Peaches, did you see him?'
'Who?'
'The gorgeous hunk sitting by the window. The one who's got the earring and that sexy tattoo.'
'For heaven's sake, Miranda, he looked as if he hadn't washed for a week and had just got out of bed.'

'I wouldn't mind getting him back into bed, then. He's scrumptious.'

'Honestly, girl, you're hopeless.'

Quiz 18

Turning direct speech into indirect speech (see page 90)

1. Ermintrude Glop said that she was once known as the belle of Glen Tuath.
2. She said she was famous for her beautifully pointed ears and shining scales.
3. Athelstan Silverwing's ode to the loveliness of her ears won the poetry competition at the winter festival.
4. Rollo Silverwing thought that old Ermintrude flaring her nostrils at his grandfather was gross.
5. Athelstan thought that once Ermintrude was beautiful but now she talked too much.

Quiz 19

Turning indirect speech or thoughts into direct speech or thoughts (see page 91)

1. Matilda said, 'Dragons come from far and near to sample Albreda's word beer.'
2. I've forgotten to put in a teaspoonful of fly agaric mushroom, Albreda worried. It makes all the difference.
3. 'You make it too strong,' her mother always complained.
4. Rollo said, 'You never make enough.'
5. 'Albreda, this year is a fine vintage,' Grimbald complimented her, 'and one of your best.'

Quiz 20

Direct or indirect question? (see page 95)

1. I, Norbert, am the handsomest, most golden dragon on the mountain. Why does nobody love me?
2. Who told you that you were the handsomest dragon, Norbert?

3. Grimbald thought, when would Norbert learn not to be so boastful?

4. As the two dragons glared at each other, Albreda arrived and asked what was the matter.

5. Where is Ermintrude? Is she still in the wild wood communing with the dragon ancestors?

6. Will Ermintrude be back when the moon has risen over the mountain lake?

7. When does the moon rise over the mountain lake?

8. Why is it that when Ermintrude is mysterious I am rather frightened, but when Matilda is, I only want to laugh?

* It's a direct question because we see the question exactly as it was asked: 'Why *is it*...?'

9. Why it is that Ermintrude is such powerful figure among the dragons, I have not the slightest idea.

* It's an indirect question because we don't see the question as it was asked, but as it is reported to us: 'Why *it is* ...'

10. Grimbald wondered why Ranulf Forktail was such an old windbag. Was it because his father had not listened to him when he was young?

Quiz 21

Turning direct questions into indirect questions (see page 96)

1. Sundeep looked at the customer's green face and asked whether he was going to be sick.

2. The groaning customer asked where the Gents was.

3. Sundeep called out to Miranda, asking whether she had put laburnum seeds in the cake, after all.

4. Miranda told him not to be so stupid, and asked whether she would really do a thing like that.

5. Miranda wondered why Sundeep always got hold of the wrong end of the stick.

Quiz 22

Turning indirect questions into direct questions (see page 97)

1. 'Surely laburnum is poisonous?' said the lady in the corner.

2. ❤ 'It certainly is,' said Sundeep gloomily. 'Why don't you wait and see if the bloke turns green?'

* ❤ Note the authors have allowed themselves some artistic licence here!

3. The lady in the corner pushed her coffee away abruptly.

    'Are you serious?' her companion asked Sundeep.

4. Miranda fled to the kitchen and a moment later Peaches stormed out.

    'What is the matter?' she demanded.

5. 'I assure you that no part of the laburnum is allowed inside the Whole Nut Café,' Peaches told the ladies in the corner. 'Would you like a complimentary cup of coffee?'

Quiz 23

Quotations in the body of a text (see page 128)

From: *The Importance of Egg-Laying* by Grimbald Fire-Plume.

I repeat, the whole future of the dragon race is at stake and we cannot allow the decline in egg-laying to continue. The blame for this state of affairs undoubtedly lies at the door of Matilda Hurstpank, whose *Egg-Laying is a Feminist Issue* has reached the bestseller lists. I cannot believe that any sensible dragon will be taken in for a moment by Hurstpank's argument:

> One clutch of eggs should be quite enough for any
> female dragon, given that each clutch contains
> between four to eight eggs. Let her spread her wings
> a little first, find out what life is all about before she
> settles down to lay eggs. She will be a much better
> mother for having some experience of life.

It is a she-dragon's duty to egg-lay, it is what she is born to do and this modern notion of she-dragons having, as Ermintrude Glop says, 'the right to choose' is dangerous nonsense.

Mrs Glop's view is that she-dragons 'should be allowed to develop other skills'. What greater role in life could any she-dragon have than bringing young dragons into the world? My own grandmother laid twenty-one clutches of eggs and declared, 'My proudest moment came when I was awarded the gold-medal for egg-laying.' She is the true example to all young she-dragons, not the madness of Miss Hurstpank.

I am confident that this idea of so-called 'female dragons' rights' will be seen for the false argument it is. Only ugly she-dragons will follow Miss Hurstpank; truly feminine she-dragons will scorn such ways of gaining attention and do what they do best: lay eggs and safeguard the future of the dragon race.

Quiz 24

Showing titles (see page 132)

1. Miranda was reading Daphne Flowerdew's latest book, *The Karma of Herbs.*
2. Sundeep's homework was to read the article 'Spreadsheets for Individuals' this week and 'Spreadsheets for Business' by the end of term.
3. Sundeep was convinced that *Biker's Blues* was the best movie ever.
4. Neil asked Peaches to go with him to the organic food seminar at Hoddletone Hall.
5. The first session was called 'Whole Food or Horrible Food?'.
6. All through coffee, the sound system played 'Strawberry Fair' over and over again.
7. The sound system was clearly broken, so Neil made them call Events Noise Ltd, the suppliers.
8. Miranda was proud of her new title, Acting Manager, even though it was only for two days.
9. Neil told Peaches that his two favourite operas were *Don Giovanni* and *Tosca.*
10. He told Peaches wistfully that in *Don Giovanni* every woman on the stage falls in love with Don Giovanni at some point during the opera.

* The first *Don Giovanni* uses italics because it is the name of the opera. The second mention of Don Giovanni does not need anything because it refers to the character.

Quiz 25

Quotes within quotes (see page 134)

1. 'I love those old Frank Sinatra songs,' said Miranda dreamily. 'My favourite is "I've Got You Under My Skin".'
2. 'My mum likes musicals,' said Peaches. 'She made me take her to *Porgy and Bess* and she sang along to "Summertime". We nearly got thrown out.'
3. 'My Great Aunt Flora got thrown out for singing, once,' said Miranda. 'She told them, "What's the point of being old if you can't be embarrassing?".'
4. Sundeep chipped in, 'Kids can be embarrassing, too. My little brother writes songs called things like "Hello to Sunshine" and "My Pyjama Panda". But the worst one is "Sundeep's My Special Hero".'
5. 'You poor chap!' exclaimed Neil in sympathy. 'Do you actually let him perform "Sundeep's My Special Hero"?'
6. 'Can't stop him,' said Sundeep mournfully. 'The *Gazette* wrote an article about him called "Brotherly love in Bagshaw Close".'

Quiz 26

'So-called' or not? (see page 136)

1. Arabella was determined that Neil should take her to the dance, and after three hours of her 'gentle persuasion', he was almost ready to cave in.

* The writer is hinting that, in reality, Arabella's arguments are anything but gentle.

2. Peaches was coming round to Neil. She no longer called him Neil 'Hopeless-but-he-Tries' Findlay. ✔

* Nicknames inserted like this always take inverted commas; lots of boxers (and gangsters) in particular use this style.

3. We will 'clean' your carpets. Satisfaction 'guaranteed'. ✘

* Wrong use: The writer obviously wants to emphasize 'clean' and 'guaranteed' and that's what he thinks he has done. Unfortunately, to the knowledgeable reader, the use of inverted commas makes it mean: we will do something to your carpets which we call cleaning but you probably won't agree and if you complain we will weasel out of it.

4. ❤ After a weekend with the Aquarian Starburst Dreamers, Miranda found 'enlightenment' and spent a morning realigning the café tables to pick up 'cosmic vibrations'.

* ❤ Personal viewpoint: Here the writer uses inverted commas to suggest that Miranda's behaviour is something of a joke. Without the inverted commas, the writer would be taking Miranda's view completely seriously.

Quiz 27

Topic sentences (see page 143)

1. The moment Neil accepted Arabella Castle's invitation to her birthday party, she rushed out and bought the sexiest dress in a slinky red satin with a plunging neck-line. She talked her father into having a marquee on the lawn and then booked the Hot Rocket Band to play. She would make sure that, before the evening was out, she had showed Neil that they were right for each other. **Her plan to become Mrs Neil Findlay was looking good.**

2. Peaches was competent in most ways: she was efficient, intelligent and good at dealing with the customers. **Her one weak spot was mice.** She had never liked them and had taken great care about the kitchen hygiene at the café. When, therefore, she saw a mouse scuttling across the floor late one evening as they were closing, she shrieked and jumped up on to a chair, where she wobbled precariously on her high heels.

3. **Neil stepped in and took control.** He took one look at the mouse and saw that it was a field mouse. It must have come in from outside, he decided; he'd noticed a small hole by the back door earlier. He made a note to ring the Council Pest Control in the morning, ordered Sundeep to plug the hole with a bit of wire wool, dropped a tea towel over the frightened mouse and released it outside.

4. Peaches got down from the chair and slumped on to one of the kitchen stools. She rummaged around for the cooking sherry and

poured herself a large glass. **Peaches hardly ever drank and the alcohol went straight to her head.** She began to hiccup. She tried to stop but it was no good. In between fright and hiccups she started to giggle. Within a couple of minutes she was hysterical and when Neil came in she was laughing, crying and hiccuping all at the same time.

5. Neil could never find the right words when talking to Peaches, or the words he did say came out all wrong. She was so quick and bright that she made him feel like a clumsy clodhopper. Whenever she came into the room he found his heart beginning to beat faster and he felt light-headed and breathless. **In short, every time he saw her, Neil found himself tied up in knots.**

6. **This time, things were different.** After releasing the mouse, Neil came into the kitchen, pulled Peaches up from the stool, put his arms round her and held her tightly. He began to tell her how beautiful she was and, gradually, he could feel her sobs quieten. Eventually Peaches was silent. Then she looked up and gave him a watery smile. Neil felt his heart turn over.

Quiz 28

Organizing your material (see page 145)

[6] The death yesterday of Athelstan Silverwing brings to an end an ancient tradition of dragon-bat co-operation. Every evening, before the bats left his cave in Ben Eldris, he would breathe out a huge plume of flame to frighten away predators hoping for an easy meal as the bats took their evening flight.

[2] In return for his fire-breathing, the bats brought back honey nectar from the moonflowers on Ben Eldris. Silverwing claimed that the honey nectar contributed to his long life and health.

[4] Silverwings are unusual in having four nostrils, the top two are capable, with practice, of producing sound at a very high frequency and it was by this means that Athelstan Silverwing communicated with the bats. He learnt the art of bat-whistling from his grandfather. Although he encouraged his children and grandchildren to follow in his footsteps, none of them have done so.

[7]　　His eldest grandson, Rollo Silverwing, told our reporter: "Yeah, I can whistle with my top nostrils if I want to. It's good for keeping off the midges. But there's no way I'm living in a damp cave talking to a load of bats."

[1]　　In spite of his love of traditional ways, Silverwing was a forward-looking dragon and supported she-dragons' equal opportunities. Matilda Hurstpank said of him: "When I first began to lecture on she-dragons' rights, Athelstan taught me voice production. I owe him a lot. He will be much missed."

[5]　　In later years, he was well-known for running the Beltane Festival, which he did with great efficiency. Silverwing also introduced a number of exciting new events at the Festival, such as the first years' wing-flapping competition.

[3]　　Athelstan Silverwing was born an only dragon to elderly parents in Bats' Cave, Ben Eldris, Caledonia. Although he went to Cumbria as a young dragon and trained as a scale-polisher, his heart was always in Ben Eldris, and after his wife died and his dragonlets had grown up, he returned there. He leaves four sons and a daughter. He was 243 years old.

These are our choices and why we made them:

— The best opening paragraph, which says that Athelstan Silverwing is dead and explains why he is important, is paragraph 6.

— Paragraphs which clearly go together are 6 and 2, as 6 says what he did for bats and 2 says what they did for him. We think paragraph 4 should follow because it explains what special quality Athelstan had for the business of dragon-bat co-operation.

— Paragraphs 4 and 7 also go together, as 4 talks about his grandchildren and 7 introduces a quote from one of them.

— We chose to put paragraph 1 next, followed by paragraph 5, because paragraph 5 seems to be a bit later in his life, as it says 'In later years'.

— The best summing up paragraph is 3.

Quiz 29

Removing irrelevant information (see page 147)

Note: we have put brackets round the bits which are off the point.

Been thinking of my three favourite ways to seduce the ladies. Hm, difficult choice. I think they have to be: over a meal, in a gondola, and at the theatre or opera. They are all good, but each must be carefully matched with the lady. [My friend Lorenzo says that I am wasting my time — but, poor fellow, he is nowhere near as successful as I am.]

The meal, ah! the meal. First, the wine must be carefully chosen. For my money, there's nothing to beat a fine champagne. The taste lingers on the palate and slips down like velvet and the bouquet alone is enough to make her think of love. [Lorenzo, the greedy sot, drinks himself under the table, even when with a lady. No wonder I seduced his wife so easily.] Next, some black olives to pop into her mouth. Then some poultry. Once she has nibbled at a leg and you have fed her with tasty morsels of breast, she will be squirming and giggling. Quails are good. They are small and you can suck the juice off her fingers.

Then there's the gondola. The night is dark and starry and the wind balmy. You hand her into the gondola, taking care to squeeze her fingers lightly. You sink down on to the soft cushions. The lady feels safe; she can see out — but not be seen. The gondolier sings softly — well paid, you may be sure. [Stefano, the Sicilian gondolier, knows all the gossip; it was he who told me about the duke suffering from piles.] Your arm goes round her and she gives a squeak, which you ignore. Such protests are for form only. You kiss and caress her, undoing the small buttons slowly. By the time you have reached your palazzo, she's soft and melting like a honey cake.

In winter, a box at the theatre or opera is as good as a gondola, and warmer, too. Nobody disturbs you and the music enhances the mood of love. [A box is ideal for writing poetry, too. You need to remember to bring a small lantern, quill pen and ink, and paper. I've often found it most inspirational.] For ladies, the technique is much the same as in a gondola. Move your chair close to her and, after allowing some time for the music to awaken her amatory feelings, you will soon be engaging in delicious familiarities. The music will drown out her moans and sighs. Some boxes have a divan at the back so that you may finish the business in comfort. If you time it right — not difficult for a man of my accomplishment — then, as the music swells to climax, so do you — and your fair companion, too, naturally.

Quiz 30

Setting out a business letter (see page 152)

Note: There is an element of choice here. We have put the numbered points in what we believe is a suitable order. Our principle here was first, sell them the idea; then tell them what it costs. You might take a different view.

Heading: *Gourmet Menu*
Paragraph One*: What is on offer*
>   10. gourmet menu starts Tuesday 12 June for the rest of that week
>   6. complimentary glass of champagne on arrival

Paragraph Two*: Food*
>   4. fully organic
>   1. Sole with a mousseline of home grown fennel and local elderflower wine.

Paragraph Three*: Additional facilities*
>   5. new room available for large groups
>   8. we can cater for special diets
>   2. for allergies, etc., we need to know dietary requirements in advance.

Paragraph Four: *Price*
>   3. £25 a head
>   9. 10% discount for parties of 8 or over

Paragraph Five*: What to do next*
>   7. bookings to miranda@thewholenutcafe.co.uk or telephone ...

The letter

The letter might read something like this. As we have already seen, in business letters the paragraphs are usually separated by a double space, and there is no initial tab or indent:

Whole Nut Café
The Peebles
Easter Findlay

[to all customers from the Easter and Wester Findlay Gourmets' list]

June 2, 20---

Dear [Name of Gourmet member]

Gourmet Menu

I am writing to let you, as a member of the Easter and Wester Findlay Gourmets' Society, know that the Whole Nut Café will be introducing a special gourmet experience for the week beginning Tuesday 12 June. All our guests during that week will be welcomed with a complimentary glass of champagne.

Everything at the Whole Nut Café is fully organic. A typical dish from our gourmet menu is sole with a mousseline of home grown fennel and local elderflower wine.

We have recently opened a new room for large groups, so why not bring a party? We are also happy to cater for special diets, food sensitivities etc. We ask you kindly to let us know your dietary requirements in advance.

The price of this gourmet experience is only £25 a head. Additionally, we are pleased to offer a discount of 10% for parties of 8 or more.

To book a table, please email your requirements to miranda@thewholenutcafe.co.uk or telephone ...

We look forward to welcoming you.

Best wishes / Yours sincerely,

Miranda Pimbury
Whole Nut Café

Further Reading

Austen, Jane, *Emma, Persuasion, Pride and Prejudice*
Hemingway, Ernest, *A Moveable Feast, For Whom the Bell Tolls*
Keynes, Ralph, *The Wit and Wisdom of Oscar Wilde*
Kipling, Rudyard, *If, Smuggler's Song*
Orwell, George, *Collected Essays*
Partridge, Eric, *Usage and Abusage: a Guide to Good English*
Pratchett, Terry, *Discworld* series
Shelley, P.B., 'Ode to the West Wind'
Waugh, Evelyn, *Scoop*
Wodehouse, P.G., *Very Good, Jeeves*

Other books which you may find helpful:

Gowers, Ernest, *Plain Words*
Fowler, H.W., revised by Sir Ernest Gowers, *Modern English Usage*
A good dictionary, such as Chambers or the Oxford English Dictionary
A good thesaurus, such as *Roget's Thesaurus*

Other books you may find fun, if you're now hooked:

Bryson, Bill, *Mother Tongue*
Burchfield, Robert, *The English Language*
Truss, Lynne, *Eats, Shoots and Leaves*

We also recommend the Campaign for Plain English
http://www.plainenglish.co.uk/, particularly if you're
working in business or the public sector.

Index